W9-BIT-495

THE IDEA CATALOG

Jerry Jones, Editor

Lamppost Library & Resource Center
Christ United Methodist Church
4488 Poplar Avenue
Memphis, Tennessee 38117

SINGLES
Ministry Resources

DAVID C. COOK PUBLISHING CO.
COLORADO SPRINGS, COLORADO 80918

SINGLES MINISTRY RESOURCES is a division of Cook Communications Ministries International. In fulfilling its mission to encourage the acceptance of Jesus Christ as personal Savior and to contribute to the teaching and putting into practice of His two great commandments, Cook Communications Ministries International creates and disseminates Christian communication materials and services to people throughout the world. SINGLES MINISTRY RESOURCES provides training seminars, a national convention, a journal, and resource materials to assist churches in developing a ministry with single adults that will encourage growth in loving God and each other.

The Idea Catalog
Compiled and edited by Jerry Jones

©1993 by David C. Cook Publishing Co. All rights reserved.

Published by David C. Cook Publishing Co. Unless otherwise noted in the text, no part of this publication may be reproduced in any form without written permission from the publishers.

Scripture in this publication is from the *Holy Bible: New International Version* (NIV), Copyright © 1973, 1978, 1984, International Bible society, used by permission of Zondervan Bible Publishers; the *New American Standard Bible* (NASB), © The Lockman Foundation 1960, 1962, 1963, 1968, 1971, 1972, 1973, 1975, 1977; the *Revised Standard Version Bible* (RSV), copyright © 1946, 1952, 1971, by the Division of Christian Education of the National Council of the Churches of Christ in the USA, used by permission, all rights reserved; *The New Testament in Modern English* (PH), J. B. Phillips Translator, © J. B. Phillips 1958, 1960, 1972, used by permission of Macmillan Publishing Company; the *New King James Version* (NKJV), copyright © 1979, 1980, 1982, Thomas Nelson Inc., Publishers; and the *King James Version* (KJV).

Those who assisted with the editing and production of this book are JoAnn Hill, Kim Hurst, Steve Rabey, Jean Stephens, Debby Weaver, and Steve Webb.

Cover illustration by Burton Morris, represented by Creative Freelancers.

Printed in the United States of America.

ISBN 0-7814-5038-1

10   9   8   7   6   5   4

Contents

Introduction

GET OUT OF THE RUT

Is your singles ministry in a rut? Do you find yourself resorting to the same old activities, the same Sunday school class topics, worn-out leadership techniques . . . ? If you do, then you probably feel bewildered and even discouraged. You may even feel that your ministry has lost some of its impact.

Well, cheer up! Help is on the way. Your friends and colleagues in ministry from all over the country have teamed together to encourage you! Their message is this: Take a fresh look at the strengths and resources of your group and see new ways to add life and excitement to your ministry.

- Johann Gutenberg looked at the coin punch and the wine press in a totally new way, and invented the moveable press and moveable type.
- Nolan Bushnell, in 1971, looked at his television and thought, "I'm not satisfied with just watching TV. I want to play with it and have it respond to me." Later, he created "Pong" . . . which started the video game revolution.
- Thomas Edison, Henry Ford, and others remade the world, using existing materials and resources.

Nobel Prize-winning physician Albert Szent-Gyorgyi put it well when he said, "Discovery consists of looking at the same thing as everyone else and thinking something different." This has been true for many inventors, and it can be true for you, too!

This book is filled with scores of ideas generated by people in singles ministry, just like you, who looked at old problems, worn-out activities, age-old issues, and thought of new remedies, fresh ideas, and up-to-the-minute solutions.

Leafing through the pages, you will see that singles from North, South, East, and West have faced many of the same questions you have in your ministry. You'll see that singles leaders from many denominations have struggled with the same issues you have. But you'll also notice, and undoubtedly be encouraged, that this wide variety of singles and singles leaders have found successful ways to deal with those common issues. (Many of the suggestions in the following chapters were submitted to the "Fresh Ideas" section of *Single Adult Ministries Journal*. If the original source of an idea is not known, acknowledgment is given to that publication.)

The ideas in this book are presented by topic, from advertising and promoting your group to releasing your group members to serve and witness Christ's love in the community. The ideas range from the silly (see "Biff and Buffy Olympics," page 83) to the challenging (see "Warren Village: A Unique Community for One-Parent Families," page 102). In between you'll find all sorts of ideas for social activities, service projects, stimulating group discussions, group travel, interpersonal relationships, and much more.

Whether you've hit a dead end in your singles ministry or you and your group are charging ahead full speed, you'll find page after page of useful information in the chapters that follow. So, sit down, pull up a footrest, get out your highlighter, and start reading what your colleagues have to say about how you can add new life to your singles ministry!

Jerry D. Jones
Editor

YOUR IDEAS ARE WORTH UP TO $100!

If you have ideas that have worked well in your own singles ministry, we want to let others know. We are already collecting ideas for future additions of The Idea Catalog and would love to have your input. If we use your idea, we will pay up to $100. Please send a thorough description of your idea (along with your name, church, address and phone number) to:

IDEAS
Singles Ministry Resources
P. O. Box 60430
Colorado Springs, CO 80960-0430

ONE

Advertising and Promotion

A GOOD TIP . . . AND A WAITER/WAITRESS CARD

Single adults frequent restaurants often. And in many communities, the majority of the waiters and waitresses are also unmarried. Here is a creative idea to encourage your single adults to reach out to the single restaurant employees in your area.

Encourage your singles to leave a card (see below), along with a good tip—after being friendly and courteous to the server throughout the meal. This card expresses appreciation, reflects special interest and attention to their profession, and invites them to participate in your singles ministry. This type of target group advertising and outreach can be highly effective, especially with single adults.

Distribute an adequate supply of these cards to your singles. The typical single adult probably eats out at least twice a week. When you multiply that by the number of singles in your group, there is the potential for tens or even hundreds of prospects touched within a week's time. Imagine the impact also of a waiter/waitress continuing to see, week after week from different people, these cards left on the table—it raises the visibility and enhances the impression of your church and singles ministry.

What if you're not sure your server is single? Look at the ring hand without being obvious. The risk of being occasionally wrong is worth the impact of more often being right. Most married servers would not be offended anyway. A good tip covers a multitude of blunders! Besides, you could print on the card, "If you are not single, I appreciate your service and would appreciate your passing this card to a colleague."

Front of Card When Folded

Inside of Card When Opened

We'd like to return the favor
and serve YOU!

Hundreds of single adults just like yourself have found a place in West Palm Beach where they are guests of honor. We offer a full menu of opportunities for you to make good friends, enjoy new challenges, and try a fresh and healthy approach to successful single living.

For more information and a brochure describing our activities and purpose, contact

Back of Card When Folded

SINGLE ADULTS
First Baptist Church
of West Palm Beach
7101 South Flagler Drive
West Palm Beach, FL 63403
(409) 560-2342

**Thanks to: the Singles Ministry, First Baptist Church
of West Palm Beach, West Palm Beach, Florida**

REACH OUT WITH CREATIVE FLYERS

How do you communicate to the nonChristian singles in your area? Are you catching their attention? Are you speaking in a language that might address their interests, "hot buttons," and felt needs?

Here are some suggestions to consider:

1. Get two or more of your creative-thinking singles together to brainstorm some flyer ideas. How can the information be creative and interesting, not stuffy? (If you have people in your group who work in advertising or marketing, make sure they're a part of your brainstorming team.)

2. Once you have a few ideas, invite some nonChristian singles out for coffee and ask them for feedback. Do your ideas catch their interest, or do they turn them off? Explore their thoughts and perceptions. What kind of messages would appeal to them? Keep in mind who your "customer" is, who you are trying to reach.

3. Fine-tune your ideas as needed, based on the feedback you've received and the specific ministries you offer. Make sure your flyers create interest and help nonChristians see that you are fun, enjoyable people to be around. Then have your flyers printed.

4. Distribute these flyers creatively. Where in your community can your target audience best be reached? At large exhibits and conventions heavily attended by single adults? At popular hangouts or health clubs where you might be able to get permission to distribute your flyers? Apartment complexes? Give flyers to the singles in your church to place on office bulletin boards and in doctor's offices. Explore all the possibilities.

Not only will flyers like these help attract singles to your meetings, but they will also increase the community's awareness of your group. This in turn makes it easier for your singles to invite visitors because they will have heard of your ministry. Furthermore, those really needing ministry will know how to contact you.

Here are two creative examples of what one church did.

WALK ON WATER

For FREE lessons call
854-7600

Or come in person Friday evenings to
CAREER SINGLES

A single adult group designed for
- Fun, interaction, activities
- Singles in their 20s
- Singles interested in pursuing the spiritual parts of their lives

You are invited to keep dry on Friday nights at 7:30 p.m. with over 150 other singles.

(A map showing how to get to the church)

South Coast Singles
(Church address)

FOR A FREE LIFT

Call
854-7600

Or better yet come Wednesday evenings to the
SINGLES CONNECTION

A single adult group designed for
- Fun, interaction, activities
- Singles in their 30s and 40s
- Singles interested in pursuing the spiritual parts of their lives

Currently 125 singles are getting a lift from the work-a-day-grind on Wednesday nights at 7:30 p.m. Come and join us.

(A map showing how to get to the church)

South Coast Singles
(Church address)

The "Walk on Water" flyer (a play on increasing one's faith) was primarily geared to younger career singles. The "For a Free Lift" flyer was geared more to the older single who might be down, hurting, and struggling.

Thanks to: South Coast Community Church, Irvine, California

SPREADING THE WORD ABOUT YOUR DIVORCE RECOVERY

If you have a divorce-recovery seminar or ministry, produce a descriptive brochure on your ministry—including brief information on the various topics addressed in your seminar—and send it to all area attorneys, counselors, churches, newspapers, and singles on your mailing list. Also, provide a quantity of brochures to the divorce court, and distribute them at community events such as the annual health fair.

By using these creative approaches, you can broadcast your ministry to the people who need it most: people who are hurting from the pain of divorce and have not made contact with your—or anyone else's—church.

Thanks to: First United Methodist Church, Wichita, Kansas

START A SINGLES SHOWCASE

If you want to let others know about your singles group, don't just toot your own horn; form an entire orchestra!

Each year for the past several years, singles groups and resource organizations in one city—about 60 groups in all—have joined forces to present a Singles Showcase. This day-long singles information fair, held on a Saturday, gives all area singles groups and other related organizations a chance to describe their services, programs, and resources to the 1,000-plus singles who attend. To assure a big turnout, the event is publicized in area newspapers and other media.

Consider this cooperative effort in your area. In addition to informing singles of what you have to offer, you will get the chance to meet some of your colleagues in singles ministry.

Thanks to: Central Singles, Central United Methodist Church, Phoenix, Arizona

PROMOTION THROUGH PERSONAL ADS

Have you ever scanned the personal ads in your local newspaper or singles publication? If so, you've seen some ads that are interesting or funny, some that are sick, and many that show singles reaching out for a lasting relationship, love and caring.

You can use the personal ads to promote your group's activities. One group used the personals for a "teaser" campaign to promote the showing of Harold Ivan Smith's *One Is a Whole Number* film series (a popular film and video for single adults, available through Gospel Films). The key to the teaser approach is to give the audience enough to arouse their interest, but not enough information to allow them to make a negative decision.

Here's that campaign in a nutshell.

- FIRST AD
  Ad placed—one month before the film series began.
  Number of days ad ran—seven.
  Ad copy—"Harold is coming."
- SECOND AD
  Ad placed—twenty-four days before the film series began.
  Number of days ad ran—ten.
  Ad copy—"Harold says, one is a whole number."
- THIRD AD
  Ad placed—fourteen days before the film series began.
  Number of days ad ran—seven.
  Ad copy—"If you want to hear what else Harold has to say,
  be there March 11."
- FOURTH AND FINAL AD
  Ad placed—seven days before the film series began.
  Number of days ad ran—seven days (the final week).
  Ad copy—It carried complete information about who Harold was, what
  the film series was about, dates, times, location, and a phone number
  for further information.

Throughout the campaign, curiosity ran high. In fact, it ran so high that people in the paper's classified ad office refused to place the second ad until they were told what was going on.

You can do a teaser campaign, too. All you need are:

- Catchy ideas for the series of ads.
- Enough money to pay for the ads (classifieds are one of the cheapest ways to advertise).
- Someone to answer the phone calls during the final week.
- A trained, prepared staff to handle the wide variety of needy, unchurched people who may respond to your ad campaign.

Consider using the personal ads for your next promotion.

Thanks to: Reno Christian Fellowship, Reno, Nevada

THE DOLLAR BILL ATTENTION-GETTER

Here is another flyer that has been used with success. Place them where single adults are most likely to find them: laundromats, grocery stores, health clubs, pet stores, etc. Use the back side for your advertisement. You are certain to get people's attention.

Front of Flyer When Folded (Intended to look like currency folded in half.)

Flyer When Unfolded (Actual size would be the same as a dollar bill.)

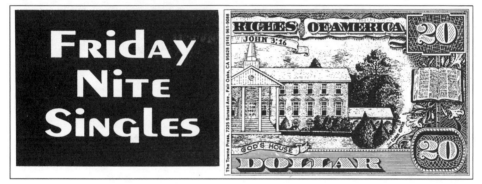

The inside copy for one singles ministry flyer reads: Friday Nite Singles, "The Christian Alternative." The place where singles come together to relax after a busy week and unwind and focus on the Lord Jesus. There is a time of worship and praise as we sing choruses and study God's Word. Then we have an extended period of fellowship, complete with a variety of activities (volleyball, table tennis, movies, pizza nights, and hay rides, etc., plus food and snacks). Activities vary throughout the year. And it's FREE! Once a month there is an exciting concert. It's a great place to meet other singles from our area and develop new friendships. Call or write for a current calendar. Join us every Friday at 7:30 p.m. (The address and phone number are also given.)

NOTE: *Before you use this idea, make sure you check the laws concerning the printing and reproduction of look-alike currency.*

Thanks to: Friday Nite Singles, Arcade Baptist Church, Sacramento, California

REACHING THE NEWLY DIVORCED

What happens to people as soon as they're legally divorced in your city? Wouldn't it be nice if they heard about your singles ministry?

Some singles ministries are pioneering just such an effort. Through an agreement with the local judge's office, a brightly colored card is attached to each divorce decree. The card informs the newly divorced person of the support and sharing available through the church single adult ministry. Here's a sample text:

SAVE THIS CARD

You may not need it right now, but the (your ministry name) singles group may be just the place for you. We offer single adults a caring family, hot coffee, fun and fellow-ship, child care, Sunday brunch, and discussions on divorce and grief recovery.

For complete, no-strings-attached information about our group and our weekly activities, please call (representative's name) at (phone number). Or contact the church office at (phone number).

You may also want to include a map to your church on the back of the card.

This idea will not be accepted by all judges, but some are anxious to give people a hopeful response to their new divorce dilemma. (You may even want to talk with one or two judges before printing the card to see what wording they would most likely approve.)

You can also distribute your cards through the local "Welcome Wagon" and other community service agencies. Furthermore, since every divorce is recorded in the courthouse, you can often get the names—and sometimes addresses—of the parties to any divorce action. Consider getting this list each month and then sending each person a letter or invitation. This is often the time when people are most open to your friendship and to spiritual support and guidance.

**Thanks to: Singles and Singles Again,
Central United Methodist Church, Decatur, Alabama**

JUST A CALL AWAY

If you have a large singles ministry with a lot of visitors, you may want to implement a singles telephone contact line.

It's as simple as going down to the local electronics store and buying a phone answering machine for your singles ministry. Next, you need to keep the messages up to date. Include details on programs and activities for the coming week. Make sure callers' questions are answered promptly. And keep your phone bills paid at all times!

Thanks to: The Single Adult Fellowship, Raytown, Missouri

"WHAT'S PLAYING AT THE MOVIES?"

Perhaps you've considered buying advertising space in the local newspaper for an upcoming singles event and wondered which section is most appropriate. Should you ask to have your ad appear on the religion page? The city beat? The local events page?

One group has had fabulous results placing their ads in one part of the paper you may not have considered. They insist that their ad appear on the movie page, along with the "R" rated movies. Singles leafing through the movie ads have responded well to this healthy alternative.

Thanks to: First United Methodist, Orlando, Florida

ANSWERING MACHINE BILLBOARD

Do you get angry when you call someone on the telephone and get that frustrating message, "No one is home right now, so leave your name and number and a brief message"?

Well, some singles ministers are turning that darned machine into a ministry communications vehicle. Listen to what one leader told us: "I wanted to go to a movie but didn't have anyone to go with, and I didn't feel like going alone. Since I'm on the program staff of our singles ministry, I thought it would be fun to try some creative ways to get a group together. So I spent the afternoon calling people who had answering machines and left messages concerning the movie, time, and theater location. That evening I stood in the lobby waiting to see who would arrive. Eight of our single adults showed up, and we had a great time!"

So, instead of getting angry, get creative. Use the answering machine to network, set up meetings, and communicate with your people. You can even tell people to expect messages about scheduled events and work out the details on their answering machines.

Thanks to: College Hill Presbyterian Church, Cincinnati, Ohio

TWO

Building Community

BIRDS OF A FEATHER FLOCK TOGETHER

Building a strong sense of family and community is one of the healthiest things your church can do. This is especially important for your ministry with single adults. Here's one creative idea that may help you effectively develop the concept of family in your singles ministry. (Consider calling it "All in the Family.") Here's how it works:

1. Divide your single adults into "family units" of twelve people or so. The groups will work best if the people in each unit live in the same geographic area.

2. Recruit two singles—a man and a woman—who are willing to be small-group leaders, the "parents" of this group.

3. Encourage each family unit to meet once or twice a month. The focus should not be on huge, organized parties but on low-key "normal family life" times where genuine fellowship can be facilitated. Family activities can range from Bible or book studies to potlucks or donuts and coffee in the morning on the way to work. They can also include bowling or activities where singles bring their actual family members who live in the area—children, parents, siblings—for a larger group get-together. Be creative. The sky's the limit.

4. Once a quarter, schedule a big family reunion at which all the families meet together as one large group. This is the time for "adopting" new people into families that have openings and for forming new families.

This "All in the Family" ministry can be an excellent way to help meet the need for more personal relationships. Here are some ideas for your family groups:

- If a person is hospitalized, it's only natural for family members to be caretakers in that situation.
- Family members could carpool to church or other group functions.
- Have a round-robin volleyball tournament at your quarterly "big event" and allow each family to make up a team. (This can help build camaraderie and team spirit within each family group.)
- Celebrate one another's birthday or other special times and events.
- Have a family picture taken. (You might even want to stage a contest in your singles ministry for a creative or unusual family portrait.)
- Take a family vacation or outing.

Encourage each family unit to be creative in living out what it means to be a family.

Thanks to: Single Point Ministries, Ward Church, Livonia, Michigan

BUILDING HEALTHY SMALL GROUPS AROUND SPECIAL INTERESTS

Here's an effective way to keep life and health in your small-group ministry:

Find solid coleaders. Head up each small group with a male/female coleadership team. This distributes the responsibility and makes both men and women feel comfortable with the leadership.

Leaders commit to six-month terms. Nobody wants to lead a group forever. But the group needs stable leadership and a vehicle for changing leadership. In this plan, leadership rotates every six months. If a group member is unhappy with the way things are run, his or her chance is coming soon.

Design groups to serve. Have each set of group leaders select a specific area of service and outreach that will be its focus for the six-month term. Some of these common interest groups may include: street ministry, convalescent home ministry, prison visitation, church renewal, prayer and Bible study, orphanages, and so on. The number of possible common interest groups is limited only by the number of interested participants.

Build groups around common interests. Traditionally, small groups have been formed geographically. However, your groups may be more loyal, cohesive, and committed if they are built around common interests and ministry desires. Ideas for developing special interest groups are found in the section below, "Developing Special Interest Groups."

Thanks to: The Church on the Way, Van Nuys, California

DEVELOPING SPECIAL INTEREST GROUPS

People who experience or enjoy similar situations appreciate the opportunity to get together to share insights, issues, concerns, and ideas. These special interest groups

Lamppost Library & Resource Center
Christ United Methodist Church
BUILDING COMMUNITY / 4488 Poplar Avenue
Memphis, Tennessee 38117

can be an excellent way for you to attract nonChristian singles in your community as well as provide a framework in which relationships can grow.

Here's a brief list of several groups you may want to consider starting in your ministry:

- Single parents of young children
- People beginning new or different careers
- The unemployed
- Writers
- Movie buffs
- Backpackers
- Painters
- Bicycle enthusiasts
- Antique collectors
- Scuba divers

All you need is two or more people who share an interest and have the energy to start a group. To begin, find the most popular special interests in your group or community, then allow these special interest groups to serve as a bridge to ministry.

Thanks to: *Single Adult Ministries Journal*

THANKS FOR THE MEMORIES

Does your group have an official photographer? Do you have someone who carries a 35-millimeter or video camera to every event, capturing those rare moments on film so your entire group can look at (and even laugh at) them later?

Nothing beats a slide show or video production—set to appropriate music—for rekindling fond memories of an event or outing. And if you do a community service project, "before" and "after" slides remind everyone of how much you accomplished.

Here's how to make it happen:

1. Get one or two members of your group to volunteer as the official photographers. Find people who like photography or video as a hobby. You may even want to appoint an official videographer. With the growing number of people owning video cameras today, you may be able to find someone in your group who would love to provide a "video show" in place of slides or in conjunction with slides. This is an excellent way to plug your media buffs into the ministry and produce a lasting legacy of your people and events.

2. Have your photographers take pictures at every major event throughout the year.

3. On one or more occasions throughout the year—year-end is a perfect time—set the slides or tape to appropriate music and have a show for your group. This review of the group's events is not only a sentimental and group-building tool for your regulars; it also helps show visitors what your group is all about.

Thanks to: Single Purpose Ministries, St. Petersburg, Florida

HELPING COUPLES MEET SINGLES

Have you ever wished the married couples and single adults in your church were better acquainted? Here's an excellent idea to help make that happen.

Hold your singles ministry leadership and planning meetings in the homes of various married couples in your church. In addition to prayer, planning, study, and leadership training, this provides an opportunity for a variety of married couples to get a positive, inside look at your singles ministry. It also allows your single adults to get better acquainted with couples.

If your couple-hosts really want to go the extra mile, they could serve your group a meal (or dessert) or help organize a simple potluck dinner. This idea should help your singles connect with various couples in your church family.

Thanks to: First Church of the Nazarene, Indianapolis, Indiana

SHOWING YOU CARE—ENCOURAGEMENT CARDS AND SECRET PALS

All of us hunger for encouragement. This can be especially true for those who have experienced pain and loss. You've seen church pew prayer cards, haven't you? Well, encouragement cards work on the same principle, except they allow people to visually tell of their love and concern for one another.

Follow these three steps to help your singles encourage one another.

1. Get encouragement cards printed (three-by-five cards work well). Each week when your group meets, distribute the cards by placing one on each chair (or give them to each person as he or she enters the room).

2. Include a time after the teaching for people to pray for others in silence and then to jot a short message on their encouragement card to someone in the group that comes to their mind. (These cards can either be placed in offering plates or dropped in a box near the door.)

3. During the week, the encouragement team (two or three volunteer leaders) mail or deliver the cards. (If you have an extra-large group, you might want to have the cards distributed in person at the following week's meeting, mailing only to those who are absent.)

Learning to be an encourager is a long process, but the encouragement cards are a tangible tool, something you can go back and look at, again and again.

For a variation, try encouraging from behind the scenes. Being a secret pal to someone in need of encouragement is uplifting for them and rewarding for you.

1. Distribute a three-by-five-inch card or handout to each person in the group. Have everyone put his or her name, address, and phone number (both home and work) on the card.

2. Collect the cards and put them in a box. Have each person draw out one name. That person should be encouraged in a creative, secretive way during the coming week (or month).

Some secret encouragement ideas include:

- Cut out letters from a newspaper or magazine, glue a message on a card, and mail it to your pal during the week.
- Send a bunch of daisies to your pal's office.
- Bake a cake and leave it on your pal's doorstep.
- Send a cassette tape with a creative message of encouragement on it.

At the following meeting, provide an opportunity for individuals to share how they were encouraged. (If things go as expected, you'd better allow a long time for people to share their joy and surprise at the encouragement they received.)

Thanks to: Northwest Bible Church, Dallas, Texas; and The Christian and Missionary Alliance Church, Salem, Oregon

PRAYER CARD REMINDERS

Have you ever noticed how people use phrases without really meaning them? Think about "How are you?" or, "Have a nice day!" Unfortunately, many people use another phrase rather loosely: "I'll pray for you." Often, they don't follow up with prayer.

Here's a way to make sure members of your group are reminded to pray for one another. At the beginning of each meeting, place a three-by-five-inch index card or sheet of paper on each seat. The copy reads as follows:

PRAYER CARD

I will remember to pray for: _____

About: _____

_____

During this week!

During the meeting, encourage everyone to look around the room and think of someone he or she feels especially impressed to pray for during the upcoming week. (If your single adults feel comfortable doing so, they may even want to ask the person if there is anything in particular that he or she would like to have remembered in prayer.) To make sure the prayer cards don't get buried and ignored, encourage your people to place theirs in a prominent location. Some suggestions follow:

- On the mirror they look into in the morning.
- Taped to the front dash of their car, thus allowing them to pray for the person on the way to and from work.
- Taped to their television or stereo, so they will remember to pray before letting themselves "veg out."

The prayer cards can be a great way to enhance community, to develop a sensitivity to the many needs in your singles group, and to encourage praying for one another.

Thanks to: First Baptist Church, Texarkana, Texas

GETTING YOUR MENTAL EXERCISE WITH A READING GROUP

If your group is like others, chances are many of your leisure activities focus on sports or other physically oriented activities. You may be surprised to find that many in your group would be interested in spending some of that group time participating in something a little more cerebral than physical. Several leaders have found that reading groups provide singles with a great forum for discussing ideas and making new friends. Others have reported that their quieter members, who sometimes shy away from boisterous physical activities, are drawn to the reading groups.

Here are some tips to help you get started:

- Meet one or two times each month. (You can meet at an area restaurant or at one of the group member's homes.)
- Have group members take turns selecting the book to read and discuss. (Books selected can be secular or religious. It's surprising how often the discussion will turn to spiritual issues, regardless of the book.) By rotating who selects the book, people are challenged to read what others are

interested in, which means they will sometimes read books they would not normally select on their own. Thus, they learn from and about each other; they stretch and challenge themselves.

• Spend approximately half of the group session specifically discussing the book. The remainder of each session might be spent discussing spin-off topics or whatever else comes up.

This group can serve a wonderful purpose in helping people get to know one another better by building friendships. It can bring together a group of people who probably would not have gotten together otherwise due to divergent interests or shyness. It can be both stimulating and fun.

Thanks to: Calvary Evangelical Free Church, Essex Fells, New Jersey

SECRET SIBLINGS

Here's a program that allows and encourages single people to do something special for someone of the opposite sex without the misunderstandings of romantic overtones. It's called "Secret Siblings," and it matches single men to a "sister" and single women to a "brother" by random drawing.

This program is designed to be strictly voluntary. Only those in the group who have indicated a willingness to participate are included. Consequently, those involved have a sufficient degree of enthusiasm and interest to accept the responsibility for their secret sibling.

Each participant is encouraged to pray for his or her "sibling" regularly, send anonymous note cards of encouragement, leave flowers or a bag of groceries at the front door, and so on.

The identity of the secret siblings is kept secret for a number of months. Then on a designated day, the identities are revealed. Some groups reveal the identities on Christmas. At a big Christmas party, each person brings a small gift for the secret sibling, at that time revealing his or her identity.

(To help compensate for an imbalance in either men or women, ask some of your people to take a second brother or sister.)

Give it a try. Secret siblings may give your singles an opportunity to express their kindness and caring to one another in a nonthreatening manner.

Thanks to: One Plus, West Side Christian Church, Wichita, Kansas

THREE Ws FOR MEN

Tell some men your group is going to focus on the three Ws, and they may think you're talking about wine, women, and wild times. They would be 33 percent correct. "Women" is one of the three Ws featured in a unique single men's covenant group. The other two are "walk" and "work."

The concept behind the "Three W" covenant group is accountability. Men often remark that they need more than mere attendance at church, or even involvement in a singles group, to keep on track. Many men believe that an all-male accountability group is the best way to make sure their lives are being transformed by the truth of the gospel.

No accountability group can cover everything in a person's life, but the three Ws of women, walk, and work are three key areas of a man's life. A weekly men's group focusing on study and honest discussion concerning the three Ws helps provide structure for meetings, Bible studies, and for the contact the men have with each other outside the confines of the group.

In addition to a regular study time together, encourage the men to pair up and keep in touch by phone at least once through the week with questions such as these: "How consistent are you being with your quiet/devotional time?" (walk), "How did you make God known at your job this week?" (work), and "Are you maintaining godly relationships?" (women).

Thanks to: Perimeter Church, Atlanta, Georgia

THREE

Evangelism and Outreach

HOW TO FIND SINGLE ADULTS
WHEN BEGINNING A NEW MINISTRY

So, you're just starting a singles ministry and you want to know where to locate single adults in your church or community? Here are four places to start.

1. Place a survey in your church bulletin to get the following information from each single adult in attendance: name, address, phones (home and work), marital status, age group, vocation, and place of employment.

2. Ask everyone in your congregation to provide the same information on singles they know who live in the area (including family, friends, coworkers), but who do not regularly attend church.

3. Visit with the person responsible for the high school/college ministry in your church, requesting the names of those who have graduated but no longer regularly attend. Find out why they aren't attending. Have they moved away, are they attending another church, or have they just "dropped out"? Follow up.

4. Contact your local "Welcome Wagon" chapter or local businesses for names and addresses of single adults who have recently moved into the area.

With this list of names you will have a good picture of both those singles already involved in your church as well as the potential ministry with single adults living in your community. Put them all on your mailing list and keep them informed about your new (or growing) ministry. Call them by phone or visit their home to extend a personal invitation and to get acquainted. Continue reaching out in love and soon you may have to begin a new building fund!

Thanks to: *Single Adult Ministries Journal*

FRIENDSHIP BREAKFASTS

What happens to the people who visit your church's singles Sunday school class? Do they disappear into the ozone, never to be heard from again? Sponsor a friendship breakfast, and more of them may come back!

During each Sunday school class, make sure every visitor is given a coupon for a free breakfast. (You may want to hold this visitors' breakfast once a month—or more or less often—depending on how many visitors your group has.)

Make sure a good core group of your regular singles will be at the breakfast to spend time with the visitors.

You can meet in a neutral place such as a restaurant, or in someone's home (which is usually more warm and friendly, but may be harder to find and more intimidating to a visitor). A monthly friendship breakfast can be a good experience for your members as well as for those people who take the sometimes difficult step to visit a new group.

Thanks to: Baptist Sunday School Board, Nashville, Tennessee

A MINISTRY BEACHHEAD

Everybody loves going to the beach. With a little effort, some of your singles (or your ministry as a whole) can combine fun and business at a house on the sand with a powerful beach outreach. Here's how.

Recruit several single adults to put up money for rent on a spacious beach house—within easy driving distance—for the entire summer season. (For those not near a beach, consider a condo or cabin in the mountains or on a lake.)

These investors are considered shareholders, and shareholders have the privilege of making reservations ahead of non-shareholders. (They can usually receive their rent money back at summer's end plus a small profit from the rental income realized throughout the season.) The shareholders are responsible for the organization and upkeep of the house during the rental period.

Select a house manager. It could be a schoolteacher who wants to earn some extra money during the summer, or someone between jobs. The house manager lives at the house full time during the summer, coordinating use of the house facilities, maintaining the house rules, planning Saturday evening family-style meals, and helping to plan and lead other corporate activities, such as Sunday morning worship on the beach.

Give singles from the church group the privilege of staying at the house on a first-come, first-served basis. (Because the cabin has been rented for the entire season, the fee usually will be a half to a third of the going rate for other comparable accommodations.)

The house can function successfully on many levels. Perhaps the first purpose of the house is to provide an inexpensive opportunity for your single adults to get to the beach, where they won't have to vacation alone, where accommodations are comfortable and the atmosphere is Christ-centered. The house can also serve as an outreach beachhead. Christian singles can bring friends and coworkers to the house for the weekend. In this relaxed, low-key setting, friendship evangelism opportunities will abound. Conversation during meals or the organized Bible study time can allow nonbelievers to raise faith questions in a nonthreatening environment.

**Thanks to: Ambassador Singles Ministry,
Fourth Presbyterian Church, Bethesda, Maryland**

ALTERNATIVE HAPPY HOUR

Talk about new wineskins! If you're interested in reaching today's young professional single adults, you may want to consider an "alternative happy hour." Although the piña coladas and daiquiris served are rum-less, the Alternative Happy Hour is definitely laced with a powerful message of Christianity directed to the young professional set. Here's what you'll need to get started:

A place. Try renting a comfortable, easy-to-reach local hotel lounge that doesn't currently have a well-attended happy hour. Consider scheduling your happy hour beginning late afternoon through the evening, Monday through Friday. Or possibly just Wednesday through Friday. Explore the possibilities that will work best in your situation.

Sounds. People need background music to facilitate mixing and conversation. Locate a talented, professional-quality Christian band or a qualified tune-spinner with the equipment and recordings you need.

Trained staff. Develop a core leadership team from among your singles who can mingle with the crowd, be available for questions, and who know how to communicate their faith in a natural, jargon-free way.

Promotion. Combine word-of-mouth with aggressive promotion in the entertainment and lifestyle sections of the local paper. If you play your cards right, the press may even beat a path to your door to cover this unusual story!

One Christian leader summarized the alternative happy hour idea this way: "Jesus went to the synagogue every Saturday, but that was not where He found the fishermen. He had to go to the lake. The alternative happy hour is one way of reaching today's 'fishermen.' "

Thanks to: St. Stephen's Church, Sewickley, Pennsylvania

BABY-HUGGERS NEEDED!

Increasing numbers of babies are being born to drug-addicted mothers. Because of their poor health and semi-addicted state, some of these babies are required to stay in the hospital for as long as 140 days. The nurses in most hospitals don't have adequate time to love, cuddle, and hug these babies as much as is needed. That's why baby-huggers are in demand in many areas of the country.

Some singles—many of them men—are volunteering to spend two to four hours each week feeding, walking, cuddling, and singing to these needy babies.

Without the huggers, the babies would lie listlessly in their cribs without adequate amounts of human contact. The hugs and touching help both parties; it's a warm, wonderful feeling of affection that goes both ways.

Why not make this a project of your singles group? Contact your area hospitals to learn more about the need and to let them know that your single adults want to help make a difference. There is therapy in touching, holding, and hugging, and you can provide it. This is an excellent way to reach out to needy lives—as well as to the hospital staffs who deal with these tragedies.

Thanks to: *Single Adult Ministries Journal*

EVANGELISTIC DINNER PARTIES

If it's true that the way to a person's heart is through his or her stomach, then evangelistic dinner parties may be a successful way to reach unchurched single adult professionals in a relaxed, nonthreatening environment. With singles becoming increasingly dissatisfied with the bar scene, this idea seems especially right for the times.

What is an evangelistic dinner party? Good question. The party, which can have from eight to 200 in attendance, depending on the location, involves a group of Christians who have each invited a nonChristian friend to the selected home for dinner. The evening is planned around two areas: the food theme (i.e., Italian, Chinese, Greek, etc.); and the evening's topic, which will address some "felt need" of those who will attend (i.e., changing careers, single parenting, time management, stress, loneliness, the pros and cons of adopting a child as a single adult, making decisions, etc.).

The creative possibilities are endless. A dinner party can be general in nature, or it can be planned with specific people in mind: single parents, joggers, school teachers, singles in the military, classical music buffs, writers, and so forth. It can be just for women, men, or both. It can be a small, formal, sit-down dinner or a large, informal meal around the pool. All that's needed is a common interest. A singles group of almost any size can effectively use evangelistic dinner parties.

Here are the necessary ingredients of an evangelistic dinner party:

The core team. This team might have as few as two people or as many as fifty or more. The people on this team need to be Christians with a heart for ministry. Each person needs to make a commitment to invite at least one nonChristian friend, coworker, neighbor, or social acquaintance. (The goal is to have a balance between believers and nonbelievers so the latter don't feel intimidated.)

The planning time. The core team needs to meet at least one month in advance of the dinner to plan the location, food theme, and topic, as well as to determine the special guest (see below).

The praying time. Spend time as a core team praying for the party, for those who will be attending, and for each "designated speaker." Ask God to provide natural, comfortable ways to introduce Him during the dinner conversation. Also pray for a sensitivity to the felt needs—the open doors—of those who come.

A special guest. Although this is not essential, it is helpful to invite a special guest who is a knowledgeable and respected voice on the topic selected for the evening. This person needs to be a Christian who can naturally discuss his or her faith in the context of the topic without being "preachy." Examples of special guests could be a bank president for the topic of finances or investing, a coach for the topic of health or fitness, or an attorney for the topic of child support. Who are the Christian professionals in your community—medical doctors, scientists, entrepreneurs, company presidents, CPAs, human resource managers, athletes? You can probably think of a number of people who you would like to invite to an event like this.

Make sure your special guest understands that the purpose of the evening is to have a helpful, informative discussion of the selected topic, but also to weave in a discussion about God and his or her personal faith in a natural way. (You can also designate two or three of your core team to briefly share their faith story, as the conversation allows, during the meal.)

The meal. Food is usually prepared by core team members, who share expenses. Keep the meal fun but not overly complicated. Don't feel so pressured in preparing the meal that you have little time or energy for your guests. Plan some sort of drink and appetizer or finger food, so there will be something available as soon as people arrive. Food helps people relax.

The invitation. Again, be as creative as possible. Print personalized, humorous, catchy invitations—or just make your invitations by phone. An RSVP is helpful. When you invite someone, you can simply say something like, "A few of us interested in _____ (the topic) are getting together on _____ (date) at _____ (time) at _____ (location). One of the people attending will be _____ (the special guest), and he or she really has a lot to say about _____ (the topic). Can you come? We'd love to have you be a part of this evening."

The dinner party. Allow plenty of time for introductions, conversation, and finger food as the people arrive. During the meal, discuss the announced topic. Don't be completely serious. Let the laughter be warm and welcoming.

When an opportune time comes for transition to issues of God and faith, let that transition happen in a natural way. It needs to be done conversationally rather than in an overly authoritative tone. Allow people freedom to ask questions, to doubt, to disagree. At some point in the evening, make sure at the very least that the special guest talks about his or her personal conversion experience with Christ, laying the groundwork for those who may want to know more. When done in a relaxed, comfortable environment, it makes it easy for nonChristians to ask questions.

Depending on the size of the singles ministry, numerous dinner parties can be scheduled every year in various homes throughout the church community. For unbelievers, attending a dinner party can often change their image of what it's like to be with Christians. And for many Christians, it's an opportunity to learn how to share their faith. At the dinner party—around good conversation and food, and with the appropriate group support—faith sharing can seem much more natural and easy.

The results can be exciting. One leader said, "In one of our recent dinners, with eight nonChristians present, two accepted Christ that evening and four others attended our singles Sunday school class the following Sunday. In all the times I've been involved in one of these parties, I don't know of any nonChristians who were offended or turned off or who refused to attend another function with the same group. In fact, they often comment that they've never met such a warm group of people before."

Thanks to: College Avenue Baptist Church, San Diego, California

HOT-BUTTON SEMINARS

Seminars are an increasingly popular and accepted means of reaching out to the unchurched. Most educated and career-oriented people are used to attending seminars in order to gain new and helpful insights. Your group can sponsor a seminar that appeals to the single adults in your community by addressing "hot-buttons," those topics that hold special interest for them. Any church, regardless of size, can do this.

When planning your seminar, think of a variety of specific felt needs among your target audience of single adults. Some popular topics are single parenting, divorce recovery, preparing for marriage, adopting as a single adult, sexual issues, intimacy, and time and life management. This is just a start. There are many other hot-button topics to address. Once you have selected the topics you will address, invite a qualified Christian professional from the community to lead each seminar.

If you do your homework, these seminars can be covered in the media through public service radio announcements and area newspapers. Religion page editors should be personally contacted. In addition, many business firms allow flyers to be placed on company bulletin boards. If only a few of these promotional ideas work, you have the potential to attract a sizable and largely unchurched audience.

It's okay to charge for your product. In fact, some people won't come to something free; they think it's worthless. As you plan your seminars, think about giving value to the attenders. If they get value, they shouldn't mind paying ten or twenty dollars for either one full day (preferably Saturday) or a once-a-week course that runs from four to six weeks.

Following the seminar, encourage participants to form small groups and meet for an additional four to six weeks. Have trained lay leaders lead these groups. This allows those attending to develop a "support network" and to discuss and incorporate more of the material from the seminar.

Seminars can be a most effective way of addressing single adult needs. They give you contact with those not willing to visit a traditional church group. To begin, simply look at the needs of singles in your community. Focus on finding the vacuum, then filling it.

Thanks to: South Main Baptist Church, Houston, Texas

INSPIRATIONAL RUN

Ready to get off your, uh, couch and move your body? Then sponsor an inspirational run.

A Saturday would probably work best for your 10K or two-mile fun run. Register as many entrants as possible; the more nonChristians, the better. Your goal is to bring nonChristian runners to a fun athletic event and to have them hear of the saving power of Jesus Christ.

Christian singles can invite their unsaved friends to train with them prior to the race, allowing them to spend time together and giving them an opportunity to plant seeds.

If available in your city, contract with a professional race organization that will properly mark and supervise the course, supply number tags for each participant, and provide computerized results of each runner's time. By providing these extras, you'll attract a greater number of serious runners who appreciate the opportunity to test their mettle in an officially timed race. In addition, the more casual participants will enjoy participating in all the hoopla of such a big event.

On the day of the event, each runner pays a registration fee and receives a T-shirt with the "Inspiration Run" logo. Registration fees can vary, but make sure you cover your costs and have plenty left over for prizes. Afterward, give awards to the top three finishers in each age and sex class. You can also give special awards to groups that register and run together or to people who are participating in their first such event.

When all have run the race, provide refreshments for everyone and offer a short testimony and gospel presentation by a local Christian athlete or coach.

Thanks to: Wooddale Church, Eden Prairie, Minnesota

MATTHEW'S PARTY

Most single adults ages twenty-five to thirty-five attend church only about six times a year. In an effort to reach that segment of the population, try a "Matthew's Party."

Matthew's party is based on the incident in the gospels where Matthew, a tax collector, gave a party so his "unchurched" friends could come and meet Jesus. Some groups believe we would be more effective in reaching unchurched single adults today by using the same approach.

Here's how it works.

Parties can be held during the weekend at a racquetball club, health spa, or hotel lounge. Try to provide an easy-listening band, plus food and beverages. In this atmosphere, nonreligious people feel comfortable discussing the issues of life, including spiritual matters.

Make sure key members of your group are present and that they're ready to talk—not preach. The parties attract people who don't consider themselves religious but who seek answers to their spiritual questions. They are perfect for people who want to find God without having to put up with boring sermons, offering plates, coats, ties, and politicized Christianity.

Having taken care of atmosphere and style issues, be ready to meet people where they are. In doing so, opportunities to present the gospel occur naturally.

Thanks to: B.O.O.M.E.R.S., Inc., Placentia, California

MEET ME AT THE COMPANY CAFE

Want to meet working singles where they really are? Then how about holding seminars on topics of interest to single workers in the cafeterias of large companies in your area (divorce recovery, single-parent skills, conflict resolution, etc.)? You might find local companies surprisingly open to the idea, and they may even offer to pay full or partial scholarships for seminar attenders!

Sound too good to be true? It's not. Here are some practical guidelines for getting the ball rolling.

Establish a trust relationship with area companies. When initially contacting a company, there may be a high degree of suspicion. One way to deal with the suspicion is to co-sponsor the seminar with leaders from churches of other denominations. When company officials understand the seminar represents a cooperative effort of people from various churches, they may be more willing to work with you. It may take a while to demonstrate your trustworthiness and to convince company brass that you are sincere in your desire to offer a genuine service. Work on building a relationship. After all, you're interested in working with companies over the long haul. Be patient, and hang in there.

Be service oriented versus church oriented. Approach companies from the angle of being a nonsectarian community service. Companies are often skeptical or suspicious of religious organizations wanting to use their facilities. Don't use an employee's personal crisis as an attempt to snare him or her into church. There can be no arm-twisting. Religious beliefs may be gently expressed, but never forced. Further discussion about faith issues can be done if people come to you on a one-to-one basis. (This will happen often if you maintain integrity and earn the right to be heard.) But it's something that cannot be abused. See this as a bridge-building opportunity, a way to reach out to people who may not normally attend a church.

Seize the day. Almost all companies are looking for ways to help their employees become more productive, healthy, and happy. If a person has just gone through a divorce, attending a divorce-recovery seminar will often help him or her grow, heal, and consequently become more productive on the job. What are the needs of the employees from the employer's perspective? Spend time exploring these with the company "powers that be." Then be creative in thinking about the ways you might help address those needs within the corporate setting.

Thanks to: The Good News Community, Wyoming, Michigan

NIGHTCLUB OUTREACH

If you're serious about reaching today's singles in a context that's familiar to many of them, try a nightclub outreach. Meet them on their turf.

Begin by renting the most popular singles nightclub in your area for one night every month. (Some clubs have slow business, or no business, on Sunday nights. If that isn't the case, explore a weeknight when the club is not usually open or does slow business.) Then find a high-quality contemporary Christian singing group that plays compelling music and even a positive popular song or two.

Serve soft drinks and snacks, and then, in an easy-to-understand manner, briefly share the gospel message. Be ready to respond to those asking questions or seeking spiritual help. (Have your staff wear red arm bands or some other recognizable item. This makes it easy for people to seek them out should they want to talk.) Provide training for your staff so they're prepared for the questions and spiritual needs they may encounter.

Promote your event heavily through top secular radio stations and by distributing flyers in the parking lots of all the area nightclubs during the week prior.

The nightclub outreach can be a fun and inspiring outreach for your group, helping raise awareness for your ministry and attracting singles to your church by being in their world. (One ministry had as many as 2,000 singles attend this event each month, with twenty to fifty singles making a profession of faith.)

Thanks to: Metro Church, Edmond, Oklahoma

CHALLENGING AND INVOLVING AN EDUCATED GENERATION

Today's young and middle-aged single adults (baby-boomers) are part of the most educated generation in American history. They are not willing to settle for easy answers or religious platitudes, and they require a certain degree of intellectual struggle as it relates to their faith. One way to reach thinking singles is by encouraging thinking.

Post-sermon discussion. One way to encourage intellectual interaction is to have the singles Sunday school class discuss the content of the weekly sermon immediately following the service, during your regular class or at an informal brunch or discussion group. If possible, invite the pastor to participate and offer further insights and feedback for questions raised. During the discussion time, your group may want to address the following:

- Do they agree with what was preached? If not, why not?
- How does it apply to their own life? Is it relevant?
- What are their doubts or questions?
- What are the practical implications of the message?

Don't be afraid to encourage such discussions. They are essential in a healthy, growing ministry with thinking single adults. The time can also provide a tremendous opportunity for the pastor to better understand today's single adults—their needs, struggles, questions, and doubts.

Suggesting future topics for sermons. If your pastor is open to suggestions, singles can come up with plenty of good topics. Even though these topics may not always be the central theme of entire sermons, they can easily be touched on in the context of another sermon idea.

Areas of concern to many singles are issues of transition and change, due to increased mobility and the faster pace of change. To help address such issues, sermons might include sound biblical teaching on topics such as:

- How to make a career change.
- Meeting friends in a new city.

- The pros and cons of waiting to get married (and/or having children).
- Pressures and issues for today's working women.
- How to find a sense of community in a world of change.

The challenge for pastors is to deal with issues that singles face. What better group to bring these topics to his attention than your own group?

If your church is perceived as one that deals with the tough issues in a straightforward biblical manner, singles (and many others) will be more likely to attend your services and programs.

Thanks to: Christian Focus, Woodinville, Washington

APARTMENT OUTREACH

Many churches offer divorce-recovery programs. Most hold the programs in their church building, but others combine recovery with outreach by taking their program to the people.

Some singles groups are reaching apartment dwellers by sponsoring a six-week divorce-recovery video and discussion group in the apartment club-house. (Two videos to consider are Jim Smoke's *Divorce Recovery* series and Bill Flanagan's series entitled *Rebuilding the Castle That Has Come Down*.) Apartment managers often see the program as a way to promote community and customer service, plus help minimize turnover. Some apartment managers have even let groups advertise this six-week video series in the apartment newsletter. In one newsletter, the bold print advertisement read, "No guilt, no hassles, and no charge!" along with the details of when and where the series would be held, as well as its content.

If the apartment management is suspicious of your group's identity or motivation, co-sponsoring the film series with a singles group from another denomination may be helpful. Often the manager's fears can be dispelled by demonstrating that the event is not the work of just one church.

The program has been a success among many apartment residents who have often invited other nonresidents to join them. In fact, some people have actually moved into the apartments after attending the sessions!

If you sponsor the recovery apartment outreach, you may want to have a plan ready in case people in the group express a desire to continue to meet. Some groups establish an ongoing support group, while others sponsor topical video seminars. And don't be surprised when people whose needs are being met through this group begin to attend your church.

With a nationwide estimated apartment tenant turnover of 100 percent every eighteen months, repeating the series every six to nine months may reach an entirely new group of people.

(For further information on the videos mentioned in this section and other resources, check with your local Christian bookstore or contact Singles Ministry Resources, P. O. Box 60430, Colorado Springs, Colorado 80960-0430, or phone 719-579-6471.)

Thanks to: Grace Presbyterian Church, Houston, Texas

RESTAURANT GROUPS

Get out of the church and into the eateries! That's the battle cry of those who seek fellowship and outreach in local restaurants.

Every week (or once a month) have members of your group select various restaurant locations for breakfast, lunch, or dinner get-togethers. Publicize the times and locations each Sunday, and make sure people know who will host and be responsible for each group meeting.

The main purpose of restaurant groups is to provide an opportunity for singles to fellowship with, support and encourage one another—plus eat together—during the week. But they can also serve as an excellent, nonthreatening opportunity for singles to bring and introduce their unchurched friends to the group. For many nonchurched, the groups have been a first step in helping them feel comfortable about coming to church.

**Thanks to: First-Centenary United Methodist Church,
Chattanooga, Tennessee**

AN ALTERNATIVE FOR SMALLER CHURCHES

Single adults enjoy being with other singles. If your church has a small group, consider cooperating with several other churches in your area by sponsoring a once-a-month (or once-a-week) interdenominational event. You could call it "Friday Night Singles." Several combinations of churches have done this, some averaging 200 or more singles each time, representing fifteen or twenty different churches.

(When one church seems to be running the whole show, some pastors may be less interested in encouraging their singles to attend. You may be able to allay any fears by involving people from several churches in the planning.)

Provide people with name tags as they arrive to facilitate introductions and conversation. Some of the activities to consider include: volleyball, Ping-Pong, movies, pizza nights, concerts, and hay rides, with refreshments served each time. Activities might vary with the season. In addition, you can have a time of singing and worship along with a short devotional.

This provides a great place to meet other Christian singles and to develop new friendships.

Thanks to: Arcade Baptist Church, Sacramento, California

SINGLES JOB FAIR

Your group is probably always seeking ways to let the singles in your community know you care about the total person. Since there are often many people looking for jobs, a job fair could be one of those ways. It is an excellent opportunity for unchurched single adults to walk through your doors without sensing heavy religious overtones. One church presented a free Saturday job fair using the following steps.

Developing a budget. Since the ministry had no money for this project, leaders presented the idea to one of the larger banks in the area. The bank's community relations office liked the idea, agreed to cosponsor the fair, and provided all the workshop speakers.

Attracting employers. Next, the church mailed out 2,000 announcements to area businesses, inviting representatives to rent a booth for $75. Twenty businesses responded, including organizations like the McDonald's Corporation and the Armed Forces as well as employment agencies and résumé writing services. The booth rental income covered all of the out-of-pocket expenses for posters, mailings, and other miscellaneous items.

Advertising. The church spread the word by distributing posters in many key locations, through free public-service announcements on radio, through news coverage in the paper, and by sending a flyer to each person on their mailing list.

Planning the program. The six workshops were scheduled so that each person could attend three. The workshops included: "Applications and Résumés," "Women Returning to the Workforce," and "Passing the Employment Interview," among others. Free refreshments were provided by the McDonald's Corporation. In addition, the church's singles group offered additional information about their ministry and services.

The church that sponsored this event reported tremendous results. In spite of five inches of rainfall that day, 300 people attended the event. Of those attending, 80 percent had never had any prior contact with the church! Fifteen percent had some prior contact, and only 5 percent were regular attenders of the sponsoring church. Several of the singles who attended came back on the following day to attend Sunday school for the first time. The event served not only to add new members to the singles ministry, but it sent out the word that this church cares about single adults.

Thanks to: First Southern Baptist Church, Del City, Oklahoma

LIFESTYLE MANAGEMENT CONFERENCE

An effective way to impact both your church and your community is through a singles-sponsored, community-wide "Lifestyle Management Conference."

Put the emphasis on managing—or "stewarding"—all areas of a person's life. Find effective keynote speakers to explore this topic, and round out your program with leaders from the community speaking on topics such as psychological, financial, physical, and spiritual management.

A lifestyle management conference gives singles some practical tools they can use, plus it offers them a unique opportunity to provide a service to both the church and the community at large.

Thanks to: First Federated Church, Des Moines, Iowa

MAKING NEW FRIENDS WITH FRAN

Getting visitors to your group isn't difficult. All you have to do is give free money at the door! Or you could give away a car or an expense-paid vacation to Mexico. But here's a better—and cheaper—way called FRAN.

FRAN stands for Friends, Relatives, Associates, and Neighbors. Invite all four elements of FRAN at one time, or schedule different groups for different weeks by having people bring friends one week, relatives the following week, and so on.

The key to this plan is getting your single adults excited about the idea, so they look forward to inviting people. Spread the invitation via a letter, a special brochure, or a flyer for each emphasis day.

FRAN will help you bring in new single adults. To accommodate them, you may want to plan special programs. But make sure that whatever you do will draw them back again.

Thanks to: First Southern Baptist Church, Del City, Oklahoma

CAREER LUNCH CLUB

This may be just the ticket if you want to provide an opportunity for Christian and nonChristian professional singles to meet monthly for sharing and building relationships.

There are a number of ways to go with this idea. Here are some things to consider.

1. Where do you want to meet? At the church or in a restaurant meeting room? Or do you want to meet at an informal meeting place and have everyone bring a sack lunch?

2. How often do you want to meet? Monthly? Weekly? Or how about a hybrid, where you have a big meeting once a month and smaller regional meetings every week?

3. Do you want one large community-wide lunch bunch, or do you want smaller, more intimate meetings: one downtown, one on the north side, and one on the south side?

4. Do you want speakers or do you want to see the groups led by trained lay leaders? Another approach would be to rotate lunch club members into the position of responsibility for leading a discussion or study.

The main purpose of the club is to focus on the intersection of careers and the Christian faith. (To advertise the lunch club, your flyer might read, "Bring a sack lunch and find out how a growing body of Christians is discovering new opportunities to apply their faith in the everyday work environment.") Make sure the meetings address such questions as these: How does my job relate to my faith? How can I serve God on my job? How do I handle challenges and temptations at work? You can probably find qualified speakers among Christian professionals in your community. A presentation by a Christian who has "made it" in terms of career success and public service may be a real inspiration to your career singles.

A secondary purpose of the club is to provide an environment where nonChristians feel welcome and can see the relevance of the gospel in their own lives. A lunch club can be a natural place to bring a coworker who might not be interested in visiting a church.

Most successful groups meet for an agreed-on period of several weeks, after which the group members may choose to continue meeting or to disband and form new groups.

For the singles groups that have tried it, the lunch club idea has proved to be a catalyst for new friendships, for introducing nonChristian coworkers to Christ, and for networking among peers.

Thanks to: University Presbyterian Church, Seattle, Washington

KILLING TIME TOGETHER

Most of us think an "evangelist" has to be outgoing and extroverted to be effective, right? Not necessarily! One singles ministry found that an evangelism program started by one of their most introverted members was very effective.

Two members from the singles group go to the local college campus and look for someone sitting alone, "killing time" (not reading, studying, etc.). They walk over and start a casual conversation with the person. (They have found it's best not to have two women approach a man, or vice versa.) Often those that are truly "killing time" are glad for the company.

These initial conversations generally last about two hours! During the course of the conversation, the pair tries to:

1. Develop an open line of communication leading to a friendship.
2. Determine if there are needs that the pair can meet.
3. Communicate the gospel.
4. Exchange phone numbers to set up a follow-up outing for pizza, the movies, and so on.

Since this approach is very low-key and is based on one-to-one relationship development, it seems to appeal to people who shy away from the more high-profile sorts of activities.

Thanks to: Lane Avenue Baptist Church, Columbus, Ohio

A REFUGE FOR REFUGEES

You've seen it on the TV newscasts plenty of times: A family is forced to leave their homeland and move to a foreign country. Many of these people end up as refugees in North America. But the untold story can be a ministry opportunity for your group; millions of these refugees are single adults.

Why not make it a group project of your singles ministry to sponsor one or more single adult refugees? You would be responsible for helping them find employment and providing them with housing, food, and clothing until they're able to take care of themselves financially. Another benefit would be the opportunity to share your faith with them.

Your group might find this project to be a very rewarding and challenging opportunity to become "world Christians" without leaving your city.

**Thanks to: Ambassadors Fellowship,
Fourth Presbyterian Church, Bethesda, Maryland**

TIPS FOR RESTAURANT GOERS

Many singles group activities include, or are capped off by, a trip to a restaurant for long hours of food and conversation. Unfortunately, most restaurant service staff will tell you that they dread seeing large groups of Christians being seated in their section. For many, these groups mean separate checks, demanding customers, and poor tips.

Here are some guidelines for making sure that every trip your group takes to a restaurant is a pleasure for you and a loving Christian witness to the people who work in the restaurant.

1. Ask the manager if a private dining area is available, explaining that your group may get noisy. If no such area is available, be considerate of those diners seated near you.

2. Greet the waiter or waitress with cheery words of assurance that your group understands the confusion of trying to serve twenty to thirty people at the same time, and you are willing to be patient.

3. Be ready with your selection when the server comes to take orders.

4. When the food arrives, help the server remember who ordered what.

5. Remember that the restaurant is in the business of selling food, not providing a free meeting place. Go with the intent of buying something.

6. Tip generously. If all you bought is a soft drink, tip as though you had

bought more. Remember, large groups often take twice as much time at a table as do smaller parties. With lower "turnover," the server has less opportunity to earn income from other customers.

7. Don't leave gospel tracts. Your lives will be a better witness than any tract.

8. Invite the waiter or waitress to your group's activities.

9. Learn the names and backgrounds of the restaurant personnel.

10. Pray regularly for the restaurant staff.

By following these ten steps, you can assure that your visit to the restaurant will be well-received. And, your group can reach out in love to the employees, which may even result in increasing their interest in the claims of the One whom you serve. (See also "A Good Tip . . . and a Waiter/Waitress Card" on page 13.)

Thanks to: First Church of God, San Diego, California

FOUR

Programming

BUILDING YOUR MINISTRY AROUND A "STATEMENT OF PURPOSE"
The singles ministry can become an island within the total church ministry, off on its own. A healthy ministry will be vitally involved in the life of the total church body. Here is one way to incorporate your singles ministry into the broader mission of your church.

Study a copy of your church's "Statement of Purpose." Then design each week's major function around it.

For example, here is the statement of purpose for one church:

As a dynamic church proclaiming the Word of God, we purpose to make disciples of Christ by:
1. Attracting and leading the unsaved to Jesus.
2. Encouraging Christians to consecrate themselves to God's purpose in their lives.
3. Providing a climate in which personal spiritual growth and worship occur.
4. Equipping believers for effective ministry to reach our city and beyond.

The singles ministry of this church then focuses on one of the four statements each Sunday. The first Sunday of the month, they emphasize evangelism. The class lesson includes a warm evangelistic message. The group takes no offering and no guests are asked to stand and give their names. They employ the use of drama and special music to focus on the message.

On the second Sunday, the theme is commitment and consecration. On the third Sunday, it's spiritual growth and nurture, and the fourth, service. As part of the class on the fourth Sunday, pre-selected singles stand and briefly tell about a ministry they're involved with (such as children's Sunday school, divorce recovery, missions, music). The leaders share new ministry opportunities and service possibilities with the group. Singles are challenged to give of themselves and are provided specific suggestions for service.

This is one way to effectively build a strong singles ministry around the mission of your church.

Thanks to: Skyline Wesleyan Church, Lemon Grove, California

"Q" (AND HOPEFULLY "A") NIGHT

When you want a stimulating change of pace, host a "Question and Answer Night." Everyone's welcome, but the price of admission is one written discussion question about the Christian life.

Collect the questions and read one. Have group members discuss it. (If the discussion strays into despair or heresy, you will want to be prepared to leap in with a comforting, authoritative answer.) When the group is ready, move on to the next question. At the end of the night, you may be surprised at how many answers your singles have when they put their minds and hearts together.

You may want to follow the discussion time with a Christian video that provides answers to some of life's questions.

Thanks to: Hope Lutheran Church, Fresno, California

ENGAGEMENT ENCOUNTER FOR SINGLE ADULTS

Thousands of married couples from all denominations and faiths have participated in the Catholic Church's Marriage Encounter, or some other marriage-growth weekend based on the encounter concept. But the effectiveness of this concept is not limited to married couples. It has also proved to be very valuable for engaged couples. Since 1969, Catholic Engaged Encounter has slowly spread to every state. As with its predecessor, couples from many faiths have participated.

Whether you choose to encourage your engaged (or seriously dating) couples to participate with an already established encounter group, or whether you choose to begin one of your own, the idea of helping couples make a lifetime commitment seems most valid for those in single adult ministry.

Here's how the encounter works. Engaged couples spend a weekend (Friday evening through Sunday afternoon) in a retreat or camp setting. The weekend is usually led by two married couples plus a pastor, clergy couple, or priest. (For balance in perspective, it's best if one of the leader couples has been married more than ten years, and the other couple less than ten.)

About one-third of the weekend is spent as a group discussing every aspect of marriage: money, sex, children, in-laws, and so on. The participants are encouraged to ask questions during this time. The remainder of the time is set aside so that each couple can talk privately about the group discussion, plus complete specific assignments provided by the leaders. (The assignments are usually a series of questions designed to open lines of communication.)

According to a leader involved in Engaged Encounter, "One of the rewards of this weekend is to have couples decide to postpone their marriage, or even sometimes realize they should not get married at all. We want to do everything we can to help the couple seriously think through this commitment. One of our slogans says it well: 'A wedding is a day. A marriage is a lifetime!' "

Thanks to: *Single Adult Ministries Journal*

SAYING THANKS WITH A ROSE

When you invite a married out-of-town guest or speaker to your group, consider sending roses to the mate left at home.

Sending roses—or making some similarly kind gesture—is a way for you to acknowledge the value of the mate left behind. Plus, it's a concrete way to affirm the important role the ones at home play in married ministry teams, even though these "home players" are not the ones getting all your group's attention and applause.

When a husband or wife does much traveling and speaking, the family unit has to make some sacrifices. It costs them something. Acknowledging the mate left at home with flowers is one way to recognize that cost and say, "Thanks for sharing your mate with us!"

Thanks to: First Presbyterian Church, Orlando, Florida

A "TRANSITION AND SUPPORT HANDBOOK"

Many singles face periods of transition during which they need unique personal support. Instead of reinventing the wheel each time a new personal need arises, why not create a "Transition and Support Handbook" for your singles? This booklet could be distributed to everyone in your singles ministry.

What could your handbook contain? Plenty.

Here is a suggested outline for an eight-page booklet:

- Page one: Cover and table of contents.
- Page two: A brief explanation about the purpose of the booklet and suggested places to call for those who need to talk to someone. (For example, this could include information on your church staff and any small support groups in your church.)
- Page three: A list of recommended counselors and counseling centers, plus crisis centers (to address such areas as substance abuse, physical abuse, rape, overeating, etc.).
- Page four: Resources specifically for health and for children (such as Big Brother or Big Sister, youth services, and child care).
- Page five: Career opportunities and continuing education. This could include brief information on regional occupational programs, business colleges, junior colleges, universities, plus some suggested reference books.
- Page six: A suggested reading list for growth and understanding, including some recommended books for the recently divorced or separated as well as books for personal growth.
- Page seven: A continuation of page six, with suggested books dealing with relationships, children, and single parenting.
- Page eight: A continuation of page seven, with suggested reading on widowhood, remarriage, career decisions, and pertinent legal issues.

Make the handbook available to all singles in the church, and make sure you update it periodically. Talk it over with your group members—they'll give you plenty of helpful ideas for your first issue.

Thanks to: Solana Beach Presbyterian Church, Solana Beach, California

ADOPT-A-SINGLE

Know any singles in your church? Know any families in your church? Why not put the two groups together with an adopt-a-single program?

One approach is for families to maintain an "open door" policy, where their designated single is free to come and go as he or she wants or needs. The single is free to visit, join the family for dinner, wash clothes, or help out around the house or yard. If the single adult has no children, he or she may enjoy the opportunity to babysit occasionally for the children of the family, leaving the parents free for some time away from the kids.

Another approach enables singles to actually move in with their "family," paying rent and helping care for other household responsibilities.

Both can be natural ways to incorporate singles into the broader family life of the church. And they give families a chance to serve singles as well.

Thanks to: College Hill Presbyterian Church, Cincinnati, Ohio

BREAKING THE MOLD

What are some of the traditional stereotypes about singles? What are some of the molds into which people try to cram them? This skit activity helps your group explore this topic.

Divide your single adults into groups of six or eight people. Then give each group a different stereotype of single people (e.g., they lack commitment, they have more time than money, something must be wrong with them if they're not married, they have unusually active sex drives, they're not really adults yet, they're irresponsible, etc.).

Have each group discuss their assigned stereotype. How do they feel about it? Do they think it's true or false? Have they ever been the victims of such a stereotype?

Next, have each group make up and act out a short skit that depicts their stereotype. This activity can be a great icebreaker to get people talking and working together. It also can generate a lot of laughs when the skits are performed before the whole group.

Thanks to: St. Stephen's Church, Sewickley, Pennsylvania

CREATING FAMILY CIRCLES

If your singles group is large, you face a constant challenge of facilitating community and caring among your members during Sunday school and other meeting times. One concept that can help you do this is "family circles."

Divide your singles into groups of eight to ten and ask each group to sit together around the same table (round tables work best) for the duration of a six-Sunday course. Select and train a mature leader for each family circle group. This person is responsible for helping lead discussions, greeting visitors, and following up on circle members during the week.

After the six weeks are over, allow three weeks of "free" seating before heading into another six weeks of family circles made up of new combinations of people. Try it and you'll see that the family circle arrangement creates an enhanced sense of community and a good atmosphere for interaction among the members who previously had fewer opportunities to get to know each other.

For a different twist to this idea, see "The Breakfast Club" on the next page.

Thanks to: Lake Avenue Congregational Church, Pasadena, California

THE BREAKFAST CLUB (INSTEAD OF SUNDAY SCHOOL)

Having trouble building a successful single adult Sunday school program? Here is what one ministry did after two frustrating years of trying the more traditional approach. It helped revitalize their entire single adult ministry.

(Editor's note: Before initiating the Breakfast Club their mid-week activities were consistently attracting three to four times more single adults than the Sunday school program. But since its inception, the Breakfast Club has become their most attended program [and their mid-week attendance has also grown 30 percent!]. Furthermore, only 25 percent of those who attend the BC participate in mid-week programs, indicating that the club is reaching new people.)

The BC meets every Sunday morning (during the traditional Sunday school time) for a continental breakfast, fellowship, Bible study, and prayer. The format is not dependent on a teacher but is organized around several motivated table leaders who serve as facilitators of the Serendipity Bible studies. The tables of six members function as care groups and are committed to supporting one another and to inviting coworkers and other acquaintances to join the group.

A continental breakfast is prepared and served by a different care group each week. Donations are received to cover expenses and an incentive is offered to the care group that is most attended during a twelve-week period.

The Breakfast Club concept has the potential to succeed if the following happens:

- The club membership remains committed to each other and to guests.
- The club officers recruit and train new care group leadership.
- The club gatherings exalt Christ and promote biblical fellowship.

Thanks to: The Singles Ministry, Portland Christian Center, Portland, Oregon

A DELICIOUS WELCOME FOR FIRST-TIME VISITORS

Do you have a favorite ice cream store or bakery in your area? A singles ministry in Cincinnati made it a habit to visit a popular ice cream parlor on Sunday nights after the weekly singles meeting. To help encourage first-time visitors to feel welcome they gave each of them an ice cream gift certificate and special invitation to join the group for their weekly "ice cream party." These certificates were also handy to enclose in the letters they sent out to all first-time visitors.

A singles ministry in Phoenix has another variation on this same theme. They deliver a dozen fresh-baked chocolate chip cookies to the homes of all first-time visitors.

This personal touch would be well worth considering in your ministry.

Thanks to: First Church of God, San Diego, California

DISCIPLING SINGLES

Angels and earthlings alike rejoice when a single adult makes a decision for the Lord. But what happens next? Do these new Christians get lost in—or outside of—the church?

One way to nurture new believers is to establish a singles discipleship program. It's easy to set up. Here's what you need to do.

Begin by equipping others to make disciples. Start a regular class that helps equip members of your church (single or married) to disciple new believers. Maintain a roster of trained disciplers who have completed the class.

Assign each new believer to a discipler. Follow up immediately after one of your singles makes a decision to follow Christ. Assign a discipler for a series of seven weekly one-on-one studies with the new convert.

Learn needs and struggles. The discipler will soon become acquainted with many of the needs and concerns of the single adult and should help the new believer with these challenges and teach him or her how to study the Bible for help and guidance. The older Christian will also have opportunities to talk about the importance of being an active part of a community of believers and to acquaint the new convert with the total ministry of the church.

Help for the helpers. Those who disciple others may think their role is solely one of giving. But they will receive help, too. As they become more comfortable in sharing their Christian testimony with their new believer, they will gain confidence in their ability to become a more effective witness for the Lord.

Thanks to: Colonial Woods Missionary Church, Port Huron, Michigan

DIVORCE AND REMARRIAGE PANEL DISCUSSION

Everyone is single once. But divorced people are single another time, and many of them struggle with the thorny theological issues of remarriage. One way to challenge your group members to think through the issues is a panel discussion on divorce and remarriage. A well-rounded panel for this discussion might be composed of the following persons:

- A Christian college professor, who can focus on relevant passages in the gospels.
- A person who was divorced and remarried, who can focus on God's grace, mercy, and forgiveness.
- A pastor of Christian education, who can focus on the historical and social significance of the divorce/remarriage issue from the perspective of your theological or denominational perspective.
- A singles pastor, who can focus on how the Old Testament treated divorce and remarriage.

Give the panel members from five to ten minutes each to make brief presentations on their focus areas. Then, after all panelists have had their say, ask the audience to write down questions on three-by-five cards. Have your moderator read the questions and solicit answers from different members of the panel.

A cautionary note: One qualification for panel participants is knowledge of their focus area. Another is a gracious spirit. You may want to meet with panel members ahead of time to avoid the possibility of head-to-head confrontations that may be detrimental, abrasive, and confusing to those in the audience.

Thanks to: College Avenue Baptist Church, San Diego, California

EXPLODING AGE BARRIERS

In most cases it makes sense to divide your singles classes by relevant age groupings (twenty to thirty, thirty to forty-five, and forty-five-plus are typical groupings). But it's also advantageous to occasionally bring all these groups together. One way to divide by age is to focus some programs on interest rather than age. You can explode traditional age barriers with events you might call TNT (Thursday Nights Together) or TIO (Talk It Overs). Such programs provide:

- A doorway into your singles ministry for the unchurched.
- Plenty of new opportunities for your single adults to serve and be leaders.
- A time for people who attend other churches on Sunday morning (that may not have a singles ministry) to come to your program.

Here are some things you can include in your TNTs or TIOs:

- ***Fellowship.*** Before breaking into discussion groups, begin with a large group opening, refreshments, name tag pick-up, and announcements.
- ***Classes.*** Plan classes that touch on topics that are of interest to single adults. Classes may work best in a lecture format or as informal discussions, depending on the subject addressed. Topics like these are worth considering: coping with separation or divorce, Bible study, cooking lessons, dance classes, car maintenance, household maintenance, self-defense, discussion groups on specific topics, personal growth groups, children and divorce, coping with grief, and computers. (You may want to charge a fee for each class to cover materials, the instructor, and child care.)
- ***Ideas of your own.*** You might consider a music program, sports activity, or a film followed by a group discussion.

The only limits are your group's imagination and person-power. The advantages are numerous. Give it a try, and you'll enjoy the results!

Thanks to: First Methodist Church, Wichita, Kansas

FLICK 'N' TALK (FRIDAY NIGHT VIDEOS)

The television networks have had some success with prime time movies. Maybe you can have a successful video program of your own. Here's one way to encourage your singles to get together, learn, and have some fun.

1. Publicize the time, date, place, and topic through your Sunday school classes and newsletter.

2. Rent videos that deal with Christian growth or contemporary issues. To find some Christian videos, check out your local Christian bookstore, the library, or a national company called Video Dynamics, which has an extensive collection of films and videos available for rent (call 1-800-647-2284).

3. Show the videos at a group member's home or at the church. Following the showing, allow plenty of time for discussion about the topic. (Some videos come with helpful discussion guides.)

4. Top the evening off with refreshments.

If your group is up for it, you may want to consider renting some major secular videos to ignite discussion about the values and issues that confront Christians today. For example, *Wall Street* might be a good choice for looking at the topics of corporate and personal greed. Other films to consider include *Tender Mercies*, *A Trip to Bountiful*, and *Chariots of Fire*. Your local Christian bookstore may have lists of secular videos that can serve as a lead-in to some stimulating discussion.

Thanks to: First Baptist Church, West Palm Beach, Florida

HELP FOR SPOUSES OF HOMOSEXUALS/BISEXUALS

There are many reasons people get divorces, but surveys suggest that from 10 to 15 percent of all divorces occur because one of the partners is a homosexual (or bisexual).

All divorce situations are tough, but heterosexual spouses of homosexuals usually find themselves without the support groups that may be more readily available to homosexuals in their communities. To meet this unique—but not uncommon—need, some singles groups have started support groups to deal with these subjects:

- Humiliation—learning to work through the guilt and embarrassment.
- Hindsight—learning to deal with the feelings of foolishness for not having known sooner.
- Being used—learning to deal with the pain and anger of a deceitful spouse.
- Rejection—learning to regain self-esteem.
- Sexuality—learning to rebuild a positive self-image as a sexual being.
- Effects on the family—tools to hasten the healing process and deal with other unresolved problems.

See if some members of your group are interested in starting a support group to help those struggling with a divorce from a homosexual spouse. Even though this topic is sometimes difficult to broach, you may find several in your group who identify with this need.

Thanks to: Marin Covenant Church, San Rafael, California

INNOVATIVE MEETING PLACES

Why have your group meet in the church all the time? The fact is, some of your singles might like the change of atmosphere that comes with a change of venue. If you look, you'll find plenty of places to hold your group meetings. And by meeting in new locations, you might attract new members who find it scary to venture onto church grounds. Here are a few places to consider:

- Restaurants are readily available in many cities, many of which will give you a private room if you ask in advance or meet there regularly.
- The clubhouse (also called the game room or common room) of a large apartment complex also provides spacious quarters. By advertising your meeting in the apartment newsletter, you may attract new people.
- Hotels have a lot of space—restaurants, meeting rooms, and nightclubs—which are usually empty most of the day.

Open your eyes and try some new places to meet in your area!

Thanks to: Calvary Temple, Seattle, Washington

A FIVE-MINUTE PROFESSIONAL TIP

Many of today's single adults are increasingly committed to their careers and to personal financial management. Your church can meet these singles where they are by incorporating these concerns into your meetings.

Try opening your singles meetings with practical sessions on professional and financial concerns. Invite Christian men and women in business from the area to share five-minute tips on such topics as real estate, investments, medical and life insurance, wise purchasing, and career development. This five-minute tip can be given right before the main lesson. (If there is a way to tie the tip to the lesson, so much the better.) Career-minded Christians may also benefit from seeing the positive role models of the Christian business people you invite.

Groups who have tried this approach have often seen both interest and attendance increase.

Thanks to: Calvary Assembly of God, Sarasota, Florida

A SOLUTION FOR THE "NOAH'S ARK SYNDROME"

Does your church ever have big, family-style dinners? If so, do singles feel included? Often singles feel that churches operate on the "Noah's ark syndrome": that everyone who participates in a church function has to arrive in pairs! Here's one easy way to make sure singles feel as welcome as couples.

In your announcements for the event, make sure you clearly communicate that singles and couples are invited to attend. By mentioning both singles and couples, you can help singles feel included but not patronized. When you're setting up tables for church dinners, make sure each table has an odd number of chairs and place settings. This way, there will always be a visible and welcome place around the table for people who come alone.

Thanks to: Westminster Presbyterian Church, Minneapolis, Minnesota

LOOK INTO BOOKS

If you're running out of steam—not to mention good, solid teaching ideas—you might want to start a book study in your group.

More than 50,000 books are published in the United States every year, and hundreds of good books come from Christian publishers. How can you tell which books would work for your group? You may want to consider books that have the following characteristics:

They are biblical and relevant. Look for solid scriptural teaching, but also content that is practical and hits you and your group members where they live. Your group probably has fewer eager scholars than suffering saints, so focus on giving them something that is relevant to their lives.

They are not specifically for singles. Books about singleness may have real value, but they can tend to separate singles from the rest of the church body. Instead, find books that deal with everyday issues that people face—whether they're married or single—and see how God's Word can help them. Look for books that help your singles feel like they're part of the same body as married folks.

They have a particular length. Since groups generally tackle one chapter per week, you may want to choose books that are from eight to twelve chapters in length. Make sure chapters aren't terribly long, either. Interest can wane if chapters are lengthy or if you spend more than two to three months per book.

In addition, here is another tip to help make your book study a success:

Look for ancillary products. Many books have accompanying audio cassettes or video tapes. If your book has these, you can use them as a cap-off to your study series. Or you can use portions of the tapes each week to kick off your discussions.

The rest is up to you! Once your group has settled on a book, you may now want to experiment with different group settings. Depending on subject matter, you may want to divide the class into groups of three or four to discuss the topics raised in the chapters. By discussing the subject matter, group members find ways to apply the information to their lives.

Thanks to: First Church of the Nazarene, Kent, Washington

LOST IN THE CROWD?

Are people getting lost in your weekly singles meetings? You can eliminate this problem if you follow these three steps:

1. Seat everyone at tables, and make sure each table has a sign-up sheet for name, address, and phone information.
2. Assign a host or hostess at each table who will facilitate conversation and sharing. Choose hosts and hostesses who are spiritually sensitive. With the help of the rest of the group, they can discuss the questions visitors raise.
3. Make sure your hosts and hostesses get acquainted with any visitors at the table, then follow up with a phone call or visit using the information on the sign-up sheet.

Thanks to: Single Adult Fellowship, Raytown, Missouri

CONTEMPORARY CHRISTIAN ISSUES DISCUSSION SERIES

A popular resource for meaty group discussions is the Contemporary Christian Issues series published by *Christianity Today* magazine (CT). This program utilizes issues of the magazine accompanied by student and leader discussion guides. The discussion guides provide relevant Scripture and questions for study and reflection.

You can use this resource for your group by doing the following.

- Each week, single adults are assigned a specific article dealing with a topic of current interest that demands a Christian response.
- During the week, group members read the article in preparation for discussion.
- The following week the leader guides the group through a discussion of the subject, using material provided by CT.

To keep interest running high, you may want to offer this series twice a year, with each series lasting twelve weeks or so. You may also want to limit attendance to the first twenty who sign up.

For information on the CT Contemporary Christian Issues, write Christianity Today, Inc., Contemporary Christian Issues, 465 Gunderson Drive, Carol Stream, IL 60187, or call (708) 260-6200.

Thanks to: First Assembly of God, Bakersfield, California

MEET YOU IN THE PARKING LOT

It's difficult enough for new singles to get the nerve to come out for church-sponsored events. Let's not make it harder on them by making it tough to find the meeting room.

One way to make sure your visitors feel welcome is to station greeters in the parking lot. When your church is sponsoring a singles event (or even for your regular Sunday class), make sure greeters or clearly visible signs direct strangers to the right location.

The same holds true for out-of-church meetings. For example, if your group meets for meals at a local restaurant, have greeters in the lobby or parking lot to steer people in the right direction.

Greeters can also help with follow-up ministry. During the following week, ask greeters to make contact with the newcomers, letting them know the group was happy to have them in attendance and is looking forward to seeing them back at another singles function.

Thanks to: Bear Valley Baptist Singles, Denver, Colorado

INCREASING THE NUMBER OF MEN IN YOUR GROUP

Is there a shortage of men in your group? Some guests on a recent television talk show offered this suggestion. When planning an occasional social for your group, stipulate that women who wish to attend must bring a man they are not romantically involved with (i.e., a brother, uncle, cousin, or male "nonromantic" friend).

If every woman in attendance brings a male friend or relative, it helps round out the numbers and makes for a more interesting evening socially. It may also help get more men acquainted with your single adult ministry.

Thanks to: *Single Adult Ministries Journal*

NURTURE FOR REMARRIED COUPLES

When two divorced singles remarry, many onlookers close their eyes and say a silent prayer for the success of the new marriage. Prayer is a great gift to offer any newlywed couple. Along with prayer, try these program ideas for helping second marriages succeed.

Have Sunday classes for remarrieds. People in second marriages face challenges in four main problem areas: communication, sex, money, and kids (sounds similar to first marriages!). Develop sessions that deal with these problems head-on from a biblical perspective.

Develop small group support. Place your remarrieds in small groups of three to six couples each. You may decide to have the groups meet in a home and invite a mature Christian with a stable marriage and family life to act as leader. (Ideally, the leader will be a remarried person who has enough years in the marriage to have gained success and perspective.) Groups study and discuss the topic addressed in the previous Sunday's class. Something very healthy happens when remarried couples get together and realize they're not the only ones having difficulty in a particular area. Support groups like these can provide tremendous encouragement to those struggling through the issues of remarriage.

Help parents by helping the kids. Anything you can do to provide Bible studies and supervision for children will help your over-pressured remarrieds.

Encourage remarried couples to stay involved in their group for a year, since that seems to be the critical adjustment and growth period.

Thanks to: New Hope Community Church, Portland, Oregon

PAUL'S LETTER TO SINGLES
Need a quick lesson outline for your class this Sunday? The Apostle Paul's first letter to Timothy, as outlined below, contains plenty of meaty material for singles.

- 1:1-11—Learn to face life's conflicts rather than run from them.
- 1:12-20—God can use me in spite of my past failures.
- 2:1-15—My greatest desire in life must be to please God.
- 3:1-16—I must not become a "lone ranger" Christian.
- 4:1-11—I must learn the difference between truth and error.
- 4:12-16—I must set the example in leading rather than always being a follower.
- 5:1-21—I must broaden, not limit, my circle of relationships.
- 5:22-6:19—I must keep myself pure.
- 6:11-16—Don't give up when the going gets tough!

Thanks to: Christ's Church, Roswell, New Mexico

PRACTICAL SINGLE LIVING SEMINAR
Many singles conferences focus primarily on singleness. But your conference can more effectively reach professional, career-oriented singles by concentrating on practical living rather than marital status and "singles' problems."

Try a conference with workshops that focus on these four basic areas:

- Financial management (including how to shop, cook, dress, and invest).
- Careers (legal rights, preparing a résumé, interviewing, etc.).
- Human relationships (loneliness, understanding the opposite sex).
- Time management (how to set goals and get the most out of life).

Why these topics? These are areas where singles—especially younger singles—have the most questions and concerns. Practical living conferences covering such topics will help address issues that concern them most. Or to paraphrase, instead of giving a man a fish, why not teach him how to write a good résumé? Recruit solid Christian speakers who can adequately address the topics within a scriptural framework.

Such a conference will also help build bridges between your group and nonChristians who may begin seeing your group as a source for practical, real-world help.

Thanks to: Eastside Christian Singles Fellowship of Seattle, Mercer Island, Washington

RELATIONSHIPS ANONYMOUS

Chances are you know a single person who goes from one bad relationship to another. But you don't have to stand idly by any longer. Now you can help people who have a history of dysfunctional relationships.

Several singles ministries are having success with Relationships Anonymous, which is based on the twelve-step program used by Alcoholics Anonymous. The steps are rewritten to address issues of relationship dysfunction. Issues covered include controlling and being controlled, the desperate need for some "other" person to give one meaning in life, and the compulsive personality pattern that exhibits itself in many behaviors, including unhealthy relationships.

Group meetings are similar to A.A. meetings with complete anonymity (first names only are used) and plenty of testimonies from individuals sharing successes or struggles. And Relationships Anonymous can do more than help people emotionally; it may prove to be an excellent first step toward evangelism.

If some in your group are suffering from unhealthy relationship patterns, you will want to consider R.A.

Thanks to: Central Presbyterian Church, Clayton, Missouri

"FEMINARS"—SINGLE WOMEN SEMINARS

While many churches offer "feminars" (general seminars for women), very few touch on the specific needs of the single career woman in the workplace. Single women have unique needs. Why not consider developing something programmatically to respond to those needs? Here's one approach.

Develop a seminar for your single women and focus on two specific areas:

• Providing a forum to address their specific struggles and issues.
• Helping them formulate Christian standards in all areas of life.

Among the struggles and issues you will want to explore are women and the workplace, relationships with men, parenting issues, and self-image. (You can discover topics of interest by surveying the single women in your group.)

The seminar is not an end in itself, but a way to get women together to address their unique needs. If your experience is like that of other groups, out of the seminars will spring several small-group Bible studies and support groups to help the women in their personal growth.

Thanks to: Church of the Saviour, Wayne, Pennsylvania

SINGLES "YELLOW PAGES"

Your car breaks down. Your pipes leak. You need a better job. Who you gonna call? Look in your singles "Yellow Pages."

Your singles group can put together a resource directory that will help members cope with life's trials and tribulations while building bonds of friendship and "healthy codependence" at the same time. Here's what you need to do:

1. Have each single provide his or her address, plus home and work phone numbers.
2. Next, have them list their vocational abilities (auto mechanic, résumé writer, etc.).
3. Finally, have them list hobbies and interests. These may include useful talents such as sewing or woodworking, or recreational hobbies such as skiiing or tennis. This list of hobbies provides a good bridge-builder that helps connect people with similar interests and needs.
4. Once you have the information compiled, distribute the directory to all those listed in its pages. Encourage singles to contact one another when they need a quick repair, some technical advice, or a fourth for a round of golf.
5. One church enters the information into a computer and the computer does the appropriate matching. Each participant receives a computer printout showing all the services offered or needed, plus the appropriate phone numbers. New people can be added to the system as needed.

Let no ability go unrecognized. You may even want to work with other churches in your area for a combined, city-wide singles directory. Some of the services that have been offered through this exchange have included career counseling, knitting (sweaters and afghans), house-sitting, plant care, dance lessons, typing services, help with moving, and car care.

**Thanks to: First Christian Church, Amarillo, Texas;
and Hennepin Avenue United Methodist Church, Minneapolis, Minnesota**

TAKE A TEEN TO LUNCH

Know any single adults? Know any struggling teens? Why not link up these two groups for mutual support and service by having members of your singles group provide support for your church's ministry to its own teens?

Have each adult single choose (or be assigned) a teenager in the church. Relationships work best if the single and the teen are the same gender.

The single can call the teen and arrange for opportunities to get better acquainted by taking the teen to lunch or a movie. Even something as simple as a weekly phone call will help remind the teen that someone in the church cares.

This can be an excellent way for single adults to be more effective role models and show an interest in kids who normally are struggling with tremendous peer pressure and who desperately need some adult guidance, support, and friendship. Be sure to take time to effectively inform parents in the church of the goals of the program. Solid parental support will enhance your chances of success.

Thanks to: First Church of the Nazarene, Los Angeles, California

THE CURE FOR "SOLITARY SUNDAY"

An old song says, "Saturday night is the loneliest night of the week." But many single adults find Sundays to be the loneliest time. This is especially true when leaving church alone after a warm, uplifting worship service. But it doesn't have to be that way—at least not at your church.

Here's a list of after-worship activities that your group can do to take the solitary chill off of Sundays:

- Have brunch at a local restaurant.
- Stage a "cook-in" at someone's house (sharing the costs, cooking, and cleanup).
- Have a late-afternoon discussion around the Word of God, followed by a light activity such as dining out.
- Start an afternoon talk-it-over group.
- Start one or more hobby groups.

Ask your group members which of the above activities are most desirable, and encourage them to pursue whatever they have selected. You may also want to vary your activities from time to time.

Thanks to: Solo Point Ministries, Bristol, Tennessee

THE JOB CLUB

Do you know any singles who have been unemployed in the past year? Chances are you probably do. Do you think they would be interested if your church offered a no-nonsense approach to getting a job? Would they be up for an opportunity to be with others who seek employment or wish to develop job-search skills appropriate to today's job market? Unless they're independently wealthy, the answer is probably yes.

A job club can reach singles in two important areas: the wallet and professional esteem. Its general goal is to provide Christian support and encouragement to unemployed and/or underemployed members of the church and community. Specific goals include:

- Communicating and teaching job-search skills and techniques.
- Sharing information about today's job market and how to get a job.
- Facilitating open discussion by club members about their job-search concerns and successes.
- Providing material resources useful for supporting each member's job-search campaign.

A successful job club takes planning. You need a curriculum (these are readily available through books and videos), you need a schedule, and your participants need a notebook to chart their progress. Line up community experts who can provide helpful and challenging guest lectures. Promote the club to all interested singles ministry members and their friends.

The frequency of your meetings and the length of the term depends on your group's needs (although a two-to-five month term seems best), but a concentrated effort of weekly meetings seems to work better than a club that meets infrequently. The club can also be an important source for networking and leads.

As your club progresses, make sure you allow time for the sharing of success stories and experiences from people who have taken new and exciting steps in their careers.

Thanks to: Arcadia Presbyterian Church, Arcadia, California

SINGLES SUNDAY

Help your church congregation become more aware of your single adult ministry by adding one or two "Singles Sundays" to the church's annual calendar.

This is an event that takes place during the main worship service. The service can have many components depending on your creativity and your church's traditions. Be sure to involve both the singles leader and the senior pastor. In addition, select certain singles who will briefly explain to the congregation some of the issues facing singles and how the church's singles ministry is helping address those issues. Give your congregation the perspective of both never-marrieds and formerly-marrieds.

At some point, have the single adults in the congregation stand or be acknowledged in another way. You may consider having singles act as ushers, or ask families to invite singles home for lunch after the service. Members of your church might not realize that so many of the people they see every week are a part of the church's singles ministry.

After the service (or between multiple services), host a singles fair and reception on the patio or in the fellowship hall. Invite different groups within the singles ministry to set up displays or booths about their unique ministry facets (for example, divorce recovery, single parents, singles missions trips, small support groups, and widowers ministry). Make sure they all have plenty of information to hand out to church members. Have balloons and colorful posters to help make it festive. Serve coffee, punch, and cookies.

The purpose of this event is not to be exhaustive, but to give your congregation a basic understanding of some of the ministries going on within your singles group. This event—bolstered by the senior pastor's involvement—can add to the church's overall awareness of the need and vision for singles ministry.

Thanks to: Hennepin Avenue United Methodist Church, Minneapolis, Minnesota; and Solana Beach Presbyterian Church, Solana Beach, California

TIME OUT

Some singles ministries have adapted their weekly schedule to give more time to fellowship, sports activities, leadership opportunities, and spiritual growth. If you want to create a weekly singles night, try this plan:

1. Begin at 6:30 p.m. with a light supper (sandwiches, fast food, etc.) at the church.
2. From 7:00 to 8:00 p.m., offer a selection of elective courses. One suggested course is a cooking class for those who have already perfected the food-pouch-in-boiling-water type of cookery and want to move on. Other ideas include discussions on biblical self-esteem or Christian relationship principles.
3. At 8:00 p.m., reconvene the whole group for announcements. Then open the church gym for volleyball until 10:00 p.m.

Try "Time Out" at your church. You'll see singles coming and bringing their guests. At one church, up to half of those in attendance at some Time Outs are unaffiliated with any church.

Thanks to: First Presbyterian Church, Arlington Heights, Illinois

TOUCHY STUFF IN A FISH BOWL

Here's one way to allow singles in your group to discuss whatever tough issues are on their hearts and minds. Grab a fish bowl (a bucket or other container will work) and invite people to place anonymously written questions in the bowl. Then have members of the group grab questions from the bowl and read them to the group. In order to provide confidentiality, have each person write something—even a few nonsense words—on a sheet of paper. If each person contributes something to the bowl, those who have written sensitive questions will feel that their privacy is better protected.

When given the chance to raise questions with this type of anonymity, people begin talking about sin, guilt, sex, and other topics that are usually suppressed in group-discussion settings. (It is preferable to keep the group to a minimum of ten to fifteen people to help protect people's identity.)

Here's how one person who used the fish bowl approach described the experience: "All of us have very real, personal problems. But this method of sharing has helped us realize that a shared burden is easier to bear, and that we are neither weird nor funny. We basically all have the same struggles, needs, and concerns. But because of what different ones have learned, someone usually has something very worthwhile to offer the struggling or questioning person."

One caution: The fish bowl approach may occasionally yield some issues that are better handled one-on-one with a trained counselor. It's okay to suggest counseling if such a question comes up—or, better yet, to screen the questions before they are read to the group.

Thanks to: Hermiston Assembly of God, Hermiston, Oregon

VISITORS INFORMATION NIGHT

If your singles group is serious about attracting visitors, make it a point to have a regular visitors night (or day, if that works better for your group).

The program can be like a typical meeting of your group, except that you make a special presentation to guests, giving them a better understanding of your ministry.

Follow these steps:

- Encourage all your singles to make a special effort to invite a friend or coworker.
- Show a slide or video presentation on the various activities and programs you offer.
- Have one of your leaders conduct a question-and-answer session.
- Put it in writing! Provide handouts that tell about the programs in your own singles ministry as well as information about services and activities for singles available in the community.

- Feed them! Coffee and donuts or other snacks add to the warmth of the meeting.
- Follow up. In the following week, make sure each visitor is contacted by someone from your group's follow-up committee.

Thanks to: The Christian Singles, Westminister, Colorado

REACHING OUT TO SINGLE MEN

If your singles ministry is like most, you have more women than men at your meetings. Here are two ideas for activities that may help bring more men to your singles group.

M.O.M. This doesn't stand for maternal parent-type persons. It stands for Ministry on Motorcycles. For some men, hopping on a motorcycle and getting away from it all really helps them to open up to one another and develop bonds of concern and love. But make this experience more than mere hot-rodding. Allow plenty of time for discussions around the campfire. Also, plan for light devotions and group prayer.

Risk ministry. There's nothing like a little Risk-y business to get many men talking, laughing . . . and invading each other's countries. If you're familiar with the board game Risk, then you know the hours of conversation it can stimulate.

To run a Risk ministry, all you need is one Risk game for every five players or so. Be sure to set up enough tables to have several games going at once. New games can start as soon as five people are ready to play. Have everyone pitch in from three to five dollars to cover pizza and pop.

M.O.M. and Risk have worked well for some groups, and they may work for you. But if Risk and motorcycles aren't the way to reach men in your area, keep in mind that, generally speaking, adventuresome, action-oriented, risk-taking events will help draw men. Be creative and find what works best in your community.

Thanks to: Evangelical Free Church, Palatine, Illinois

A CUP FULL OF AFFIRMATION

Affirmation and encouragement are wonderful gifts to receive and to give. Here's a handy little exercise to help encourage your singles to get in the habit of giving this gift to one another.

1. Ask your group members to sit in a circle.
2. Give each member of your group a paper coffee cup.
3. Have each person write his or her name on this cup.
4. Distribute small slips of paper to each member, one for each person in the circle.

5. Instruct each person to pass his or her cup to the right.

6. As the cups are passed around the circle, each person takes one of the slips, writes a compliment or sentence of affirmation about the owner of the cup, then drops it into the cup.

   Note: Encourage people to be sincere in what they write. Challenge them to focus on something unique and special in each person. Trite, shallow comments can hurt. If they don't know the person at all, it is better to simply say so than to make something up.

7. By the time the cups return to their owners, they will be running over with affirmations. (You might suggest that people contain their curiosity and take their cups home to read just one affirmation a day until the cup is empty.)

Although somewhat mechanical, this exercise may help to get affirmation flowing in your group. See if you can think of other ways to keep the positive comments coming in the future.

Thanks to: First Church of the Nazarene, Indianapolis, Indiana

SEVENTHIRTYSOMETHING

Since many scheduled events don't start exactly when they're supposed to, one group has decided that "If you can't beat 'em, join 'em." This particular group's Thursday night meetings are supposed to start at 7:30.

In the summertime, they have decided to offer a sort of "staggered-start" evening program. For those that want to show up right after work and grab a quick burger, there is a barbecue at 6:45. For others who want to arrive a little later, there's soft drinks and socializing. This option usually appeals to the 7:15 to 7:45 crowd. Those that don't like to spend a moment dilly-dallying can arrive sometime between 7:45 and 8:00, in time to be there for the beginning of the Bible study.

The leaders of this group have found that the casual approach to the start time is a real relief to those group members that have been fighting deadlines and traffic jams all day.

Thanks to: Coast Hills Community Church, Laguna Niguel, California

FIVE

Socials
and Special Events

THE GREAT DESSERT BAKE-OFF

Follow these steps for a tasty way to have fun, hold a friendly competition, and ingest a gaggle of calories.

Establish your entry categories. The following is an example of several categories you may want to consider:

- Beginners (those who have been cooking for a year or less).
- Most exotic dessert dish.
- The "Julia Child Award" (for best female dessert-maker).
- The "Galloping Gourmet Award" (for best male dessert-maker).
- Fanciest dessert dish.
- Best low-calorie dessert.
- Best high-calorie dessert.

Announce the date, time, and categories for your "Great Dessert Bake-Off." Allow plenty of advance warning so your people will have time to make their desserts. Encourage (and recruit, if necessary) as many participants as possible. The more, the merrier.

Those making an entry are encouraged to notify the organizers in advance. This helps with planning and also ensures an adequate number of entries for the evening. Allow people to select the category in which they will compete.

Let the bake-off begin. On the designated evening, set up a nice display area for each category, where everyone can place their desserts. Each entry is assigned a number to allow the contestants anonymity.

Put the judges to work. Judges, who are selected in advance, are recruited from the community at large. (Consider recruiting a chef or two from a well-known area bakery or restaurant, a state fair judge, and a local radio or TV personality.) Supply each judge with clipboards and sheets for each category. Make sure that pitchers of water and cups are placed at each table so the judges may regularly wash their palates.

Plan a program. While the judges are busy tasting, let the singles enjoy a program, a comedy skit, or a film to keep themselves occupied (and their hands away from all the goodies) while the suspense mounts. This can be a great time of fellowship and interaction in a festive atmosphere.

After the judges finish, ask them to tally up their choices and provide the results to the emcee, who then announces the winners. Each winner receives a gift.

Get down to the serious business! After the prizes have been awarded, the highlight of the bake-off begins as the evening becomes a dessert potluck.

The bake-off has many advantages:

- It gets people into their kitchens to test their skills.
- It can become one of the special-event highlights each year.
- People can have one big evening where they don't have to feel guilty about eating all that "decadent" stuff. After all, it's for a good cause, right?
- Food can also be a real outreach tool. Just watch how many guests show up to eat your goodies.

Thanks to: Single Point Ministries of Ward Church, Livonia, Michigan

FRENCH TOAST JAMBOREE

Here's a delicious (and economical) way to have Sunday lunch together.

After the morning service, meet in the church dining area or at someone's home. Instruct your singles to bring their favorite French toast topping (syrup, jam, preserves, honey, etc.), plus one dollar to cover the cost of the bread, milk, butter, and eggs. The toppings are easy and convenient to bring, and the price is right.

You can have a group of designated lead cookers, or the responsibility of preparing the French toast can be rotated among the single adults present—even among those who don't usually find themselves in the kitchen!

Thanks to: First Presbyterian Church, Colorado Springs, Colorado

CHALLENGE OF THE CO-ED STARS

Remember the TV show "Challenge of the Network Stars"? The show's concept was that millions of Americans would tune in to watch famous stars run track, play ball, and look gorgeous—even in their athletic outfits.

You can borrow the same concept for a big-time event of your own. Try to schedule about twenty-five events, including volleyball, softball tournaments, sack races, wheelbarrow races, an egg toss, a pie-eating contest, and much more. Then turn people loose to compete.

The only requirement is that each participant have a partner of the opposite sex in each event.

Thanks to: Eastside Christian Church, Mercer Island, Washington

AIR-BAND FEST

No, we don't think your people are teenagers. And yes, we are living in a sophisticated era. It's just that the fine tradition of air-band contests (lip-synching) is being discarded as people get older and "more cultured." Maybe it's time to have some crazy, zany fun again!

All you need is a good emcee, a sound system, and a number of air-band acts who will mouth and act out the music they are performing. The music can be humorous old fifties songs (like "Splish Splash I Was Taking a Bath"), contemporary pop and rap, or even country and classical music! The possibilities are unlimited.

Consider having a panel of judges. (Maybe you can even get your city mayor or some other area dignitaries to serve as judges.) Then give out fun awards to the winners.

For the singles ministries who have tried this, it has been a smashing success with some wonderful laughs. It's also a great way to get to know the hidden talents of people in your group.

Thanks to: Christian Singles of Central Oregon, Bend, Oregon

CLASS REUNION

Within the life cycle of a single adult ministry, people move on, get married, and/or get involved in other ministries. To help old friends keep in touch, have an annual reunion.

Host the event at a nice buffet-style restaurant that can accommodate the many people who might attend. (You may want to make reservations in advance.)

The program can consist of special music, a speaker, or a humorous skit. But one of the main highlights should be looking at slides or videos of past singles events, camping trips, and parties. Make sure to allow ample time for catching up with old friends.

Class reunions can help ease the transition process when people are leaving old friends ("family") and moving on to other stages in life.

Thanks to: Northwest Hills Baptist Church, Corvallis, Oregon

GROUP DATE NIGHT

Group dating is a wonderful way to get to know others and to nurture relationships in a nonthreatening, relaxed environment. Here's one approach to encouraging group dating with your singles.

Choose a night (either once a month or weekly) when people can meet. Begin with a catered dinner at six o'clock followed by a program at seven. The program can feature guest speakers on topics ranging from aerobic dancing to spiritual life to sexuality. Then for those who want to continue the evening, the group dating possibilities begin at eight.

Work with your group to design attractive group dating options. One group may want to go out to a movie. Another may choose to visit an all-night restaurant for coffee and dessert. Still another group might decide to go square dancing. Whatever the choices, many singles will be glad for this group date opportunity.

Thanks to: First United Methodist Church, Lubbock, Texas

GUESS WHO'S COMING TO DINNER?

One of the challenges that many singles ministry leaders face is how to integrate single adults with the rest of the church family. This church-wide, in-home dinner idea can be one way to begin the process. Here's the menu to follow:

1. Every person who wants to participate signs up in advance.
2. At the same time, house hosts are recruited for the various groups.
3. The organizers divide the people into groups on the basis of age and marital status, ensuring a good balance of older and younger, single and married in each group. The size of the groups depends on the number of people that can be handled at each host home. (Try to get from ten to twenty people in each home.)
4. About one week before the event takes place, mail a postcard to all participants, telling them which home they will visit for dinner and what food dish they should plan to bring. Here's where the fun and suspense come in, because no one knows who else will be going to any particular house, what anyone else is bringing to eat, or anything!
5. After sharing a meal together, the host family leads the group in some games, a devotional, and prayer. It is also a wonderful setting for good informal conversation. The guidelines for these activities can be prepared ahead of time and given to the host families.

"Guess Who's Coming to Dinner?" could be so popular and effective that you may want to repeat it on a quarterly basis in your church.

Adapted from the *Baptist Leader*, January 1984

MINI-VACATION ADVENTURES

Build rapport and experience fellowship through crazy, bizarre mini-vacation road trips. These quick vacations can begin Friday night after work and go through late Sunday.

To get the ball rolling, select a planning team. To make things work smoothly and to share the burden, each mini-vacation should have its own planning team, which is responsible for such things as selecting a destination and planning the meals, travel itinerary, and transportation.

When planning the destination, ask yourselves these questions: Where are some places your group has always wanted to visit? Which historic sites, national parks, recreation areas, archaeological digs, and other famous spots are within driving distance? It is usually best to keep your destination within a six- to eight-hour drive from your town or city. Draw a circle on a road map to help you see all the possible places to visit within the allowed driving time. For example, if you lived in Denver, such places as Mount Rushmore or the Continental Divide are within six hours' driving time.

These mini-vacations can demand a lot of time in the car or bus, but that's half the fun. Great fellowship and sharing take place as you travel down the highway toward someplace new and out of the way.

Many singles never really take vacations because of limited finances or because they have no one to go with. But these mini-vacations offer a great weekend adventure at a very reasonable price. To help keep expenses low, consider camping out, getting group rates at inexpensive motels, or staying in someone's home or a church basement.

Your group just might get excited about these spontaneous, unusual road trips. Try one and you'll see that short adventures can become memory-making times together.

Thanks to: Resurrection Fellowship, Loveland, Colorado

OUTDOOR ADVENTURERS

This may not be for everyone, but chances are there are several in your group with a special interest in being outdoor adventurers.

These hardy souls can get together to plan outdoor activities and events nearly every month. Activities can include canoe trips, camping, hiking, biking, and fishing. You may also plan events that include children. Some of your group's best friendships can grow out of these activity-oriented interest groups.

While the adventurers are out running around God's green earth, others may want to start some interest groups based on photography, bicycling, writing, genealogy, pottery, or stargazing. Use your imagination and find some ways for your people to get together in meaningful shared-interest groups.

Thanks to: Grace Presbyterian Church, Houston, Texas

PIZZA AND PJs PARTY

For a novel way to spend a Saturday night, consider holding a "Pizza and PJs" party, either at the church or at someone's home. Get the singles pastor or leader together with the members of the group and add the following ingredients:

- Pizza fixings and drinks (instruct people to bring their favorite toppings).
- Videos (consider fun stuff like The Marx Brothers or The Three Stooges).
- Sleeping bags and pillows.
- Toiletries and clothes for Sunday.
- Pajamas, sweatsuits, or other modest sleepwear.
- Breakfast fixings for the next morning. After all, you'll need to eat something before you all go to church together!

This pizza party will provide tasty food, fun laughs, and a chance to relive the adventure of those junior high slumber parties you remember.

Thanks to: The Westside Christian Church, Wichita, Kansas

PROGRESSIVE JACUZZI-FOOD-SWIM PARTY!

The progressive dinner has been around since Moses and his gang wandered from place to place experimenting with all the possible ways to prepare manna! Now many singles groups are giving the progressive idea a new twist by adding such elements as jacuzzis and saunas.

To have your own progressive dinner, you might do something like this: Start at house number one for appetizers and a dip in the jacuzzi. Then move on to house number two for soup and lawn darts. After that, hit house number three for salad and a sauna. The only limits are what your bodies can endure and the number of houses that have fun stuff provided to do!

What a great way of breathing new life into an already "progressive" idea!

Thanks to: Quail Lakes Baptist Church, Stockton, California

SINGLES CINEMA

Even though the home video industry has come into its own, many people still enjoy the chance to get out to the Bijou for a night at the movies. Your singles group can have fun playing host to movie-goers by cosponsoring (with one of your local theaters) a "Singles Cinema" night.

What theater personnel need to do: An hour prior to the movie, they provide a social time in the lobby with plenty of popcorn and soft drinks (maybe at a reduced price). This should be relatively easy and painless for them, plus they'll sell a ton of movie tickets!

What you need to do: Advertise the event far and wide. The theater may even be willing to help with the advertising costs. On the evening of the event, make sure your leadership team is available to mingle and build bridges with all the singles in attendance.

After the movie, invite everyone to an adjacent restaurant for amateur Siskel-and-Ebert-type reviews of the flick. Depending on the movie content, the "review" could provide some interesting opportunities for addressing values and faith issues.

"Singles Cinema" night can take some of the hassles and solitude out of movie-going, and it can do wonders to increase the visibility of your singles ministry in the community.

Thanks to: First Church of God, San Diego, California

"WHAT'S MY LINE?" NIGHT

Remember "What's My Line?" the old TV show from the fifties and sixties? No doubt you do. It was the longest-running game show in the history of nighttime network television!

The show's popularity was due to people's interest in various occupations. And you can use that interest for your "What's My Line?" night. Here's how:

1. Ask all the singles to come to an evening party dressed for the occupation they would most like to have.
2. Then, on a large display board, list everyone's real occupation, without listing their names.
3. The challenge for the evening is to go around and match up people to their real occupation.
4. Although it's not necessary, you might want to consider giving a fun award to the person who matched the most people with their correct occupations within a certain time period. (You could also give an award to those with the hardest-to-guess occupations, or to the people doing something most opposite to what they would really like to be doing, etc.)

"What's My Line?" night can encourage everyone to talk, to get better acquainted, and to find out who does what and why.

Thanks to: Solana Beach Presbyterian Church, Solana Beach, California

RESTAURANTOURING

What is "Restaurantouring"? It's a way to enjoy the fun of eating out without having to eat alone. Here's the plan:

Each month, your group visits a different restaurant, which has been selected by the group. Members make their reservations with the group's person-in-charge, who relays information to the restaurant in time for the staff to make the necessary arrangements.

You can plan your restaurantouring for any night in the month, but many find that Sunday afternoon or evening works best. Many singles say that eating alone on Sunday after church is one of the loneliest times of the week. For others, Friday night is the best time to get together for dinner with friends. In some churches, the location of the dinner is announced in the bulletin or from the pulpit, so singles visiting the church will know they have a place to go that night for a friendly meal.

Restaurantouring provides both fellowship and the opportunity to get to know many new restaurants in your city.

Thanks to: St. Luke's United Methodist Church, Oklahoma City, Oklahoma; and Pioneer Baptist Church, Abilene, Texas

SWEETHEARTS' EVENING

Many singles in your group may have formed friendships with married couples in the church. If neither the single nor the couple have children, they may find they have a lot in common and have many ways to express their friendship. But if the married couple has children, the single may sometimes find it difficult to spend time with the couple or show appreciation for the mutual friendship they share. Now there's a way for the singles in your group to express their appreciation and friendship for their married friends. They can do it by hosting an annual (or more often) "sweethearts' evening" in which single adults plan a night for the kids so the married couples can get away for a date.

To prepare, distribute or post a sign-up sheet for all married couples interested in taking advantage of this special service. The advance sign-up helps the single adults to plan for appropriate age groups and activities and to make sure they have phone numbers where parents can be contacted in case of an emergency.

The singles then plan the evening activities based on the ages of the children they will be caring for. The evening may include showing a Christian video, playing Ping-Pong, or providing various games for the kids.

Sweethearts' Evening is a great way to get singles involved with the couples in the church, as well as give them an opportunity to love some kids. And your willingness to take the children for an evening just might help promote marital bliss and stability!

Thanks to: New Testament Christian Church of Greece, Rochester, New York

TENNIS ANYONE?

One surefire way to help your singles enjoy some regular summer fellowship, plus plenty of good exercise, is to set up an ongoing tennis outing every Saturday morning at a convenient tennis court in the community.

Find two or three of your singles to host each Saturday's event, then encourage anyone interested to show up. To add some excitement, you might even organize a summer-long, round-robin tournament.

At the end of the summer, participants will have at least three benefits to show for their efforts: a tan, a better serve, and some new friends!

Thanks to: First Centenary United Methodist Church, Chattanooga, Tennessee

VIDEO INTRODUCTIONS

Video teaches people how to flatten their tummies, improve their golf swings and travel to far-off places. But can it help your singles get to know each other? You bet it can!

Invite members of your singles classes to bring pictures of themselves (and their children, if they have any) from early childhood to present. Transfer the photos to video cassette and show the different tapes at various times throughout the year. Use the videos to spotlight someone on his or her birthday or to help make your group seem a little less anonymous.

Thanks to: First Assembly of God, Clearwater, Florida

VOLUNTARY-COMPULSORY DATING

Often it seems that singles either don't date at all or feel awkward when they do. The voluntary-compulsory date night is a time when everyone can enjoy a date free of hassles, tension, and the pressures of "romance."

Plan and advertise your date night well in advance. When the night arrives, instruct each person to put his or her name in the appropriate hat, one hat for men and one for women. Singles then select their partners by the drawing of a name from the hat.

Each pair then goes out for an evening of dinner and conversation. To keep people from feeling too awkward, send them out in groups of four to six. Following the dinner, everyone can meet at a miniature golf course or bowling alley to spend an enjoyable evening with the larger group.

Some groups have found that this activity attracts a lot of single men. People really enjoy this opportunity to have some healthy fun and spend time together socially without the pressures generally associated with dating.

Thanks to: Cherry Creek Presbyterian Church, Englewood, Colorado

V-BALL FELLOWSHIP

To the die-hard volleyballer, the sport needs no defense. But some skeptics may say, "Show me what volleyball produces other than sweaty bodies and bruised knees." Combined with a fellowship meal and a brief devotional period, volleyball can produce powerful results among single adults. Here's the game plan:

1. Select a neutral place to play (possibly a boys club, health club, or YMCA).
2. Advertise this regular monthly or weekly event through a flyer, public service radio announcements, and the city newspaper's free community calendar section.
3. Have a potluck dinner, with the option that those who haven't prepared food can pay the singles fund two or three dollars.
4. After dinner and before volleyball, have a fifteen-minute devotional. (Keep in mind that there may be unchurched singles in attendance.) Introduce newcomers and announce birthdays.
5. Play ball. The physical exercise helps break down barriers and build camaraderie.

Once friendships develop, the activity serves as a drawing card, helping previously unchurched singles feel comfortable enough to go to church or a weekly Bible study.

Through this activity, several single adults have made their first contact with the church and have ultimately become healthy, growing Christians.

Thanks to: First Wesleyan Church, Bartlesville, Oklahoma

SINGLES CONCERT SERIES

If you want to plan an activity that will reap a lot of excitement (and possibly even a few bucks) for your singles ministry, sponsor a Christian singles concert series.

Your group can select professional Christian musicians (anyone from Stonehill to Petra, from Truth to Russ Taff), market the tickets, and work with others in your community to share the energy and entertainment.

Begin by having your group make a tentative listing of artists you would like to host. Then contact the artists' managers or booking agents (these names and phone numbers are often found on the lyric sheets of the artists' albums) and find out specific information about dates and costs. If you start small and grow, a concert series can become one of the big social events of your singles ministry.

Thanks to: Wooddale Church, Eden Prairie, Minnesota

MAKE BLOOD-GIVING A GROUP PROJECT

Blood means life. Why not invite your local Red Cross bloodmobile to your church some Sunday morning? By organizing a church blood drive once or twice a year your group can help raise awareness of the need for clean blood sources and make it convenient for your entire group to "give the gift of life." (You may even want to tie in a lesson on the life-giving power of Christ's blood on the Sunday closest to your group blood drive.)

Thanks to: Hope Lutheran Church, Fresno, California

BEATING THE HOLIDAY BLUES

The holidays are often tough times for singles. Thanksgiving and Christmas are thought of as "family days," and many divorced or never-married singles feel especially lonely without family members to celebrate with. Single adult ministries often plan meals or group activities to draw people together during these special yet difficult times.

But big group activities aren't the only cure for the holiday blues. As a leader, you may wish to provide a handout with additional ideas for beating the holiday blues. Here are four things you could suggest to your singles, encouraging them to take the initiative to create a special day for themselves and others.

Invite others to your home for a Thanksgiving or Christmas Day potluck. Or, if you feel adventurous, ask guests to bring the ingredients only, and get the whole gang in the kitchen preparing the meal en masse! Better still, if it's company you wish, more so than gourmet fixings, imitate Woody Allen's character in Broadway Danny Rose and serve turkey TV dinners and frozen pumpkin pie!

Spend the day by yourself, serving people. Load your extra sweaters, jackets, and blankets in your car and head out to find chilly streetpeople who might appreciate the warm clothes, or a kind chat, or hearing about the love of Jesus.

Or you might pop in unexpectedly at the home of another single friend whom you suspect is spending the day alone like you. Many singles turn down dinner invitations during the holidays because they feel so awkward showing up without a date. Your surprise visit really might brighten a lonely day.

Spend the day with others, serving people. There is bound to be an organization somewhere in your area that would love to have your help serving a Thanksgiving or Christmas Day meal to the disadvantaged.

Spend the day alone. If loneliness isn't an issue in your life, but lack of meaningful time for reflection and rest is, then use the day to slow down and privately thank God for His work in your life.

Thanks to: College Hill Presbyterian Church, Cincinnati, Ohio

MAKING NEW FRIENDS AT SINGLES RETREATS

Are you looking for some new ways to build friendships among those who attend your singles retreats? Here are two ideas to try at your next retreat.

First, at one of the meals, sit everyone at tables according to birth month. If space permits, divide each month in two so that those born the first to the fifteenth of one month are at one table, and those in the second half are at another. Retreat guests will enjoy meeting one another, and will probably remember one another's birthdays later on in the year. If your group is large enough, many singles will be seated with their "birthday twin," a new friend who shares the same date of birth!

Second, ask each person to write his or her name at the top of a blank sheet of notebook paper. Affix all blank sheets to one of the walls of the main meeting room or the dining hall. Throughout the weekend, have the others write words of encouragement and affirmation to the person whose name appears at the top of the sheet. At the end of the weekend, each person will have a page full of documentation that they're loved and appreciated!

**Thanks to: Solo Con East Annual Retreat,
Church of the Nazarene, Kansas City, Missouri**

COOKING FOR ONE OR TWO

Most recipes are written for four or more people, so singles often end up eating leftovers for a week, throwing food away, or simply not cooking at all. One way your group can address this dilemma—and have a fun event at the same time—is to sponsor a "Cooking for One or Two" class.

Contact the cooking instructor at the head office of a supermarket chain in your area. (Sometimes this person is called the Consumer Specialist or the Home Economist.) Arrange to have that person develop recipes that will feed one or two people, then come to your group for a cooking demonstration and tasting party.

In addition to learning and sampling new recipes, singles can ask for advice on cooking techniques, nutrition advice, and shopping hints. If all goes well, you may start seeing some healthier looking people at your singles meetings!

Thanks to: Bethel United Methodist Church, Glencoe, Missouri

PARTYING, FUTURE STYLE

If your group enjoys having theme dances and parties structured around a bygone era, then you've probably tried your hand at a fifties dance, complete with poodle skirts for the women and slicked-back hairdos for the men. Or maybe you've hosted a sixties dance, with flower power in evidence everywhere. Or even, dare you admit it, a seventies dance, with those awful disco outfits!

Well, how about adding a twist to your planning? Instead of reminiscing about those days gone by, why not have your group look into the future toward those days not yet here? How about hosting a zeroes party, centered around the latest fads and fashions in the first decade of the next century! In addition to wearing the latest zeroes outfits, your group will have fun planning a futuristic menu, thinking of games, and dreaming up new dance crazes!

So start planning your zeroes party now and get those invitations faxed!

Thanks to: College Hill Presbyterian Church, Cincinnati, Ohio

TAKE A GROUP VACATION

Every summer, millions of families pile into the station wagon and drive off toward the horizon for a fun family vacation. But what's a single person to do?

It's simple: take a summer vacation with your extended family of singles. Many singles ministries take their entire group on a summer vacation. The action is nonstop, the group discounts and savings can be sizable, and the only limits are your members' imaginations! (Some singles ministries have taken more than fifty singles on a group vacation!)

Begin planning early by asking interested group members to set aside a week or two of vacation time during the summer. Members who belong to AAA or travel clubs can collect travel information and estimate costs. Plan something that will interest a lot of potential vacationers: maybe a trip to a Colorado dude ranch, to a Wisconsin fishing lodge, or even to Europe.

Once you are "on vacation," plan for scheduled activities as well as free time. Be sure to use the time not only for rest, but for relationship development and spiritual growth as well. Ask various singles to lead morning devotions and evening studies throughout the vacation.

Group vacations are an excellent way to bring your singles together in new and geographically diverse ways!

Thanks to: Evangelical Free Church, Palatine, Illinois

BIFF AND BUFFY OLYMPICS

Here's a let's-have-fun-with-the-yuppie-mentality idea for an activity to try at your next retreat or party. Divide the group into teams of six to eight people and get ready for the challenge of "A Day in the Life of Biff and Buffy," a yuppie-style relay race!

Once your teams are chosen, have each one pick an appropriate team name: The BMWs, The Saabs, The Volvos, The Mercedes, and so on. Then put each team through its paces. Start by "dressing for success" (putting on and taking off a full business suit before moving to the next station). Next, it's on to "Perrier with a Twist" (pushing an empty Perrier bottle through a short course—with your nose!). Think of your own fun variations, the possibilities are limitless! How about the morning shower, taking the kids to day care, "power lunching," racquetball or aerobics after work, the end-of-the-day jacuzzi. . . .

So get ready, lace up those ergonomically designed, air-pillow insole athletic shoes, and go for it!

Thanks to: First Presbyterian Church, Colorado Springs, Colorado

VALENTINE SUPPER

Are the gentlemen in your group looking for a way to show their affection and appreciation for the ladies? A special valentine supper may be just the way to do it.

On the night of the dinner, each woman is picked up at her home by one of the men in the group, given a red rose, and taken to the home where the supper is to be held. The women are seated at the table and treated to a special dinner, prepared by the men. The gentlemen do not eat with the ladies; instead, some make sure water glasses are kept full, others stay in the kitchen preparing the dessert, while others serenade the ladies with song.

On a night when single people may be feeling left out, this valentine supper is a great way to break out of the mold, try something new, as well as communicate playfulness, affection, and selflessness.

Thanks to: St. Paul United Methodist Church, Midland, Texas

HEALTH CLUB NIGHT

How would you like to meet a lot of new people, get plenty of exercise, participate in team and individual sports, and eat good food . . . all in one evening? If this sounds good to you, then start preparing now to host a singles night at the health club. Here's all you do:

1. Contact a local health club about renting the entire facility for an evening. (The more amenities the club has, the better.)
2. Have your planning team begin making arrangements for a lot of group sports activities (basketball, volleyball, aerobics, etc.), individual sports events (tennis, racquetball, etc.), and unstructured activities (weightlifting, treadmill, exercise bikes, etc.). Plan to finish the evening with a time of worship or a brief message.
3. Make food available, either provided by the health club or by hosting a health food potluck.
4. Establish a per person cost that will cover the club rental and other costs.

5. Advertise far and wide. Unless your group is really large, you may not be able to attract enough people to keep the price low. So use this event, which is a natural ice-breaker, to introduce nonChristians and other newcomers to your group (you may even consider allowing newcomers to attend free of charge). Or contact other singles groups in the area and jointly host the event.

You'll enjoy this high-energy, low-threat friendship builder. Not only will long-time members enjoy the evening, but newer members of the group will find it easy to meet new friends. Parents will enjoy participating in an event that's as fun for the kids as it is for the adults. Perhaps best of all, this is the type of event that group members' nonChristian coworkers will enjoy attending.

Thanks to: Mercer Island Singles, Mercer Island, Washington

CHEAP STUFF

Most singles groups have their share of people in tough economic situations. If you want to be sensitive to all of your people and their various budget limitations, make sure your programming includes several events that are free or low-cost. That way, those who live on tight budgets are able to participate at least some of the time with the more affluent folks.

Here are some suggestions to consider.

Everybody loves to eat and talk around the table, but some singles can't afford going out to eat all the time. Vary your dining activities. One month have your singles brunch after church at a mid-priced restaurant or fast-food restaurant, on another Sunday share a potluck at someone's home.

Going out to the movies every now and then is great fun for your group. But movies cost more and more all the time. With the wide range of rental videos available, go that route as often as possible. You can show videos for free . . . or real cheap, like twenty-seven cents a person! If your church, or someone in your church, has a big-screen television, it even feels like a movie theater!

Remember to try some cheap stuff. The single parents and unemployed folks in your midst will really appreciate it.

Thanks to: First Presbyterian Church, Berkeley, California

SIX

Leadership

"MR. POTATO HEAD" LEADERSHIP TRAINING

"Mr. Potato Head" was a fun childhood game in which you used creative imagination and asked, "What do we want this thing to look like?" The same principle can be used with your single adult leaders when planning and evaluating your ministry's effectiveness. Have your leaders engage in some firsthand cultural reconnaissance. Here's how it works:

1. Let your leaders know you're going to have a Friday-to-Sunday brainstorming leadership retreat in a hotel located near the center of your city.

2. Before the retreat begins, compile a list of the following:

- Most popular singles bars in the city.
- Most popular health clubs.
- Fastest-growing churches that are reaching single adults.
- Other popular single adult hangouts in your area (beach, laundromat, grocery store, etc.).

3. Divide your leadership group into teams. Help them come up with a list of five to ten key characteristics to look for on this fact-finding mission. Have them ask these kinds of questions:

- Why is this particular place so popular?
- What kind of people are here?

- Are they having fun or are they bored? Why?
- What kind of people are in charge?
- What are the ages of the people?
- Are the people all professionals, all blue collar, or a mix?
- How are people dressed?
- Is it highly organized or unorganized?

4. On Friday night, send your fact-finding teams out to the bars, health clubs, and even churches that have something planned for singles.

5. On Saturday morning, talk about Friday night. What did your leaders observe? What did they learn that can help you develop a more effective singles ministry? Did they recognize any blind spots or barriers that might be negatives in your ministry? If they were starting a single adult ministry totally from ground zero, how would they do it?

6. On Saturday afternoon and into the evening, send the teams out again. Have them go to places they did not visit on Friday night.

7. On Sunday morning, send your fact-finding teams out again. Be sure to visit places *in addition to churches* where singles might congregate. This in itself can be an eye-opener. Find out what singles are doing when they are not sitting in church.

8. On Sunday afternoon, come back together to share observations and brainstorm effective ways to reach single adults in your city. Make a list of reasons why these places are popular with singles and then compare your own group and church to those characteristics. Discuss how you can implement your findings in your own singles ministry.

The purpose of the fact-finding mission is to force you and your group to face the facts and recognize some of the barriers that may be keeping singles away from your church. Take a cool, calculated look at your ministry and ask, "If we had no traditions, preconceived ideas, or rituals, what would we do to most effectively reach single adults in our community?"

Thanks to: B.O.O.M.E.R.S., Inc., Placentia, California

LEADERSHIP RETREAT WITH POOL TIME
How do you keep your leaders on the cutting edge and help them enhance their own effectiveness? Some ministry leaders recommend a one-day retreat for single adult leaders every six months.

It's simple and painless. Rent a meeting room at a hotel and spend the day in full-group and small-group sessions dedicated to brainstorming, discussing objectives, planning long-range goals, and getting to know each other better. You can also invite your senior pastor to come participate with you briefly, which helps reaffirm the church's support.

End the day by relaxing around the pool and cementing your relationships.

The leadership of your group is worth an investment of time twice a year. This is a great way to train new and current leadership.

Thanks to: First Evangelical Church of Rockford, Illinois

A LEADERSHIP COVENANT

Serving on a ministry leadership team is a serious thing. As an acknowledgment of the seriousness of the responsibility, some groups have their leaders commit themselves to a leadership covenant like the one provided below. You may want to consider using this one or one tailored for your particular needs.

MY LEADERSHIP COVENANT

1. I will faithfully serve to carry out my responsibilities throughout my leadership term of (length of commitment in weeks/months/years).

2. I will commit myself to living in community with the others on this ministry team. This means I will strive for mutual support, accountability, vulnerability, life-sharing, gift-evoking, planning for ministry, and group prayer.

3. I will attend the weekly meetings of our ministry team.

4. I will use my personal gifts regularly as a member of this ministry team.

5. I will use my material assets generously, with 10 percent of my income (a tithe) being the minimum I will give to this church in any year. (Persons not currently at a 10 percent giving level may have six months of grace to move up to that level so as not to shock their budget too severely.)

6. I will be open to God daily for my growth, in one or more of the following ways:

   a. Quiet meditation
   b. Prayer
   c. Journaling
   d. Scripture study
   e. Worship

7. I will be intentional about my personal growth and training for my personal ministry by participating in workshops, seminars, studies, and other events at this church and elsewhere.

8. I will participate in the parish/congregational life of this church.

Adapted from *Alternative Lifestyles Confront the Church* by Deane W. Ferm, New York: Seabury Press, 1983

THE "NO BUSINESS" LEADERSHIP MEETING

Remember that your primary mission is not to do the ministry, but to equip your people to become ministers. One way to help you do this is to have two separate meetings each month for your leadership team. At one of the meetings, focus on conducting the business of your ministry. At the other, focus on your leaders as persons and conduct absolutely no business.

Singles ministers who follow this plan believe the second meeting is the more important one. It is structured around interpersonal sharing in groups of two or three, prayer, and group interaction. The focus is on affirming one another's giftedness, and on building community.

The purpose is to help each of your leaders to grow. The better your leadership team functions as a growing, healthy Christian community, the better they model that to your group at large.

While it may seem like spending a second meeting on personal growth issues may be an impractical waste of time, the beautiful truth of the matter is that as you and your leadership team learn to know, trust, and love each other better, you are able to conduct your business more efficiently. Plus you may even begin looking forward to being together instead of dreading another meeting!

Thanks to: Bear Valley Baptist Church, Denver, Colorado

THE "LAUREL AND HEARTY HANDSHAKE" AWARD

For a fun play on words, try this idea as a way to recognize your volunteer leaders. Public acknowledgment and thanks are so vital for your leadership team. They help everyone in your ministry appreciate their value and importance.

THE LAUREL & HEARTY HANDSHAKE AWARD
Presented to:

Sometimes a fun certificate like this, even though it is very inexpensive, can become a coveted award. Find other creative ways to express thanks and affirmation. It's an excellent way to encourage volunteerism within your group.

Thanks to: West Side Christian Church, Wichita, Kansas

THE CORE-TEAM LEADERSHIP MODEL

Far too often single adult leaders end up with too many responsibilities and consequently burn out. This often happens because lay leaders assume responsibility for both the direction of the ministry and the logistics of the group. Here's a new leadership model that divides these leadership responsibilities into two groups, the "core group" and the "team."

The core group: This is a co-ed group of five to ten singles who accept the responsibility to lead and nurture others. They meet at least weekly for prayer, fellowship, Bible study, and ministry planning (with a focus on the big picture). Due to the high level of commitment required, membership is somewhat exclusive. This group is primarily responsible for the overall direction of the ministry. Few of the nitty-gritty details are dealt with here.

The team: This co-ed group of fifteen to twenty singles oversees the logistics of all social, ministry, and outreach events. The team focuses more on the nitty-gritty details of the ministry. While a lesser commitment is required, serving on the team has often been a natural stepping-stone to involvement in the core group. One person leads the team, serving as liaison with the core.

With this leadership model, both groups can have greater goal orientation and program ownership. Plus, this arrangement gets all the work done without "burning out" the leaders and has the added benefit of creating a grass-roots feeling of mutual support within the larger group.

Thanks to: Church of the Savior, Wayne, Pennsylvania

RECRUITING MINI-PASTORS

A mini-pastor is not a pastor who is short in stature, nor a member of your church's staff who does less than his or her share of work. Instead, a mini-pastor is a Christian single adult with the gift of compassion and a desire to help others. You have several of these in your group, although some of them may be very quiet and hard to notice. These sensitive people can be a most valuable tool in your ministry.

How does the mini-pastor concept work?

1. Mini-pastors are recruited through announcements, bulletins, newsletters, and personal contact. They are accepted only after completing an application and having a personal interview with one or more members of your leadership team.

2. Mini-pastors have the following qualifications. They are Christians willing to commit themselves to—and accept responsibility for—the ministry. They must

be concerned and sensitive to people's needs and actively seeking personal spiritual maturity.

3. Once recruited, they go through a six-to-eight-week training program for two hours a week. There, they are taught to be Johnny-on-the-spot counselors during singles activities and Sunday school. Other training might include "Christlike Counseling," "Telephone Ministry," "Active Listening," "How to Understand Depression, Bitterness, Lack of Forgiveness," and "Making New People Comfortable."

4. A twenty-four-hour phone helpline is set up at the church office with a call-transfer line. After office hours, calls are transferred to a mini-pastor's home. Mini-pastors rotate this duty. Service remains anonymous and no personal phone numbers are given.

5. Mini-pastors are identified during all activities and events by an official mini-pastor badge.

So quit looking for short people and begin recruiting some mini-pastors!

This service can provide a fleet of caring helpers for your own group. In addition, it can make the community more aware of your church's ministry as word of the telephone helpline gets around.

Thanks to: Central Community Church, Wichita, Kansas

THREE QUESTIONS TO ASK

Whether you're just beginning a singles ministry or have had one operating for a long time, here's a helpful way to keep in touch with the needs, feelings, and ideas of your singles. At least three or four times a year, invite a representative group of five to ten singles to your home for dinner or coffee. (Try to include one or two single adults who are not currently involved on a regular basis. You may learn helpful things about why some singles are dropping out.) Explain to them your interest in addressing their real needs—in being relevant—in your ministry. Then ask them these three questions:

1. How is our church effectively meeting the needs of singles now? (This helps you see things that should be continued.)

2. How is our church partially meeting the needs of singles? (This shows things you need to do more of.)

3. How is our church not meeting the needs of singles? (This shows things you need to begin doing.)

After getting your representatives' answers to these questions, you should have a clearer idea of how things are going and what needs to be changed.

Thanks to: *Single Adult Ministries Journal*

RE-EDUCATE THE CONGREGATION
ABOUT SINGLES AND SINGLE ADULT MINISTRY

Part of being a singles ministry leader involves helping the congregation and church leadership understand the value and importance of a ministry with single adults. You are a representative for the single adults in your church and community.

Here are four ideas that can help you be an effective representative and leader—as well as help those in your church to become more aware of the needs and concerns of single adults.

Awareness Exercise

Ask for fifteen minutes at the next church board meeting. Let whoever is in charge know that you are not going to ask for money, space, or anything else. All you want is fifteen minutes for two of your single adults to talk about:

- What it feels like to be single in the church.
- What they appreciate most about the church.
- Some of the specific ways they believe the church might be more effective in its ministry with single adults.

Do this several times each year. Communication and feedback such as this may encourage the church leadership to begin developing a better understanding of how to address the needs of the single adult population within the church and community.

Helping Them Get to Know YOU

If you are the singles pastor or designated leader, here is a way to build a healthy relationship with the rest of the church.

Ask if you can guest teach all (or several of) the adult Sunday school classes one time over a three- or four-month period. The purpose would be twofold.

First, let them meet and get to know you in the context of a smaller group. Let them know you don't bite.

Second, share your philosophy of ministry and why you feel a call to work with single adults. This helps maximize understanding and awareness down the road. It also can help others catch your vision for ministry.

Image Inventory (by Word Association)

Give everyone an index card on some Sunday morning as they arrive for worship. Have them write down three or four descriptive words about single adults.

Collect the cards as people leave. During the week, go through the cards, compiling a list of the most commonly used, descriptive words. On the following Sunday give a report to the congregation: "Here's what this church thinks about single adults." Then read the words used to describe single adults.

Compare them with words generally used for married couples. For example, you may often see the word *irresponsible* as a descriptive word for young singles. But that word may seldom be used to describe young or middle-aged married couples.

This exercise can help your congregation become more aware of the stereotypes—usually unjustified—that they may give to single adults.

Helping Your Pastor Understand the Need for a SAM

Many pastors and church leaders are unaware of the enormous increase in singleness in our culture over the past two decades. A good place to begin "selling" the idea of a single adult ministry is with the cold hard facts. Here are some places to begin.

Public library. Do research on recent population statistics, especially for your city, state, and region. Show your pastor and board members what a significant segment of the population singles represent today.

Other church leaders. If your senior pastor has apprehensions about the nature or need of single adult ministry, consider getting some "testimonials" from senior pastors who have strong singles ministries. Ask them about the benefits of a ministry with single adults in the local church. Share this information with your pastor and church leaders.

Resources. A growing number of books are becoming available within the Christian community that address the needs and benefits of a ministry with single adults. Check with your local Christian bookstore.

Thanks to: Christian Focus, Woodinville, Washington; and College Avenue Baptist Church, San Diego, California

(See also "Helping Couples Meet Singles" on page 26.)

SEVEN

Single Parents

SINGLE PARENT "TAX"

Many single parents are unable to attend social events and outings because of the cost and/or lack of child care. But you can do something to involve your single parents—and their children—in more special activities.

Whenever you sponsor any function that costs something for those who attend, simply charge from one to five dollars more for each ticket. The additional money is then used to buy tickets for the children who are able to go, or to help pay child-care costs for those children who cannot.

Few, if any, people will grumble about this "tax" if they know the reason behind it.

Thanks to: First Baptist Church, Modesto, California

PROFESSIONAL "ANGELS" NETWORK

LeeAnn, a single parent in your group, has just discovered an abscessed tooth and is in desperate need of a root canal. But the problem is she does not have adequate dental insurance coverage, nor can she afford to pay what it's going to cost. Unless you have an unusual ministry, you probably don't have the thousand or so dollars to fork over. So what can your ministry do?

One way to help is to set up a professional network of "angels," people who are willing to provide services for those in need for little or no cost. This idea can work in any community if you or some of your leaders simply take the initiative to get it started, then find a capable volunteer or staff person to serve as the network coordinator.

A professional "angels" network works like this:

1. Contact area professionals (doctors, lawyers, counselors, dentists, etc.) to see if they would be willing to work with two or three single-parent families in the community on a "no-charge" basis (or at reduced rate). Those who have begun this ministry have found professionals to be willing participants. In fact, most of them have said yes, even though the professionals involved are not necessarily Christians. Generally speaking, professionals enjoy helping people—that's why they've selected their "people-helping" profession to begin with! (Many even have a heart for missions, but because of their practice and family responsibilities, it's hard for them to go to Haiti, Mexico, or South America to give of their time and talent. The "angels" network fulfills their desire to give of themselves within their own practice.)

2. Request (insist) that these professionals limit this "ministry caseload" to two or three single-parent families. This minimizes their burden and helps keep them from being taken advantage of.

3. Single parents who have needs apply for help. (You could set up a three-person panel to help review and assign each case.) Based on the need, they are assigned to the professional who can best serve them.

One singles ministry helped more than 100 single-parent families over a two-year period through this network.

Thanks to: Calvin Presbyterian Church, Seattle, Washington

A "TUESDAY SCHOOL" FOR CHILDREN

Which night of the week do you have the largest singles gathering? Why not work with the children's ministry in your church and run a children's program concurrent with the singles activity?

For example, if your largest singles gathering is on Tuesday night, you could call the kids' program "Tuesday School." This special kids' program makes it easier for single parents to participate, plus it provides an excellent opportunity for the church to help work with those children who may be going through their own divorce-recovery process.

Thanks to: New Hope Community Church, Portland, Oregon

LETTER-WRITING CLUB FOR NONCUSTODIAL SINGLE PARENTS

It can be very hard for parents to maintain a consistent relationship with their children when they are separated by great distances. Yet many psychologists agree that children and parents can benefit greatly from letter writing. It can provide a means of healthy bonding and remind both parties that they are loved. But as most of us know, it can be difficult to maintain consistency when it comes to regular correspondence. That's where the letter-writing club can come in.

Once a month, have your noncustodial parents get together at someone's home for dinner and an evening of discussion and letter writing. The discussion can focus on some of the unique challenges and opportunities of being a noncustodial parent. The time set aside for letter writing helps encourage parents to be consistent.

This is also a great time to exchange creative ideas on how to effectively communicate with your child. For example, your group might want to have a theme for each of your meetings, coordinating letters, calendars, large postcards, and stickers around the monthly theme. Explore other creative through-the-mail ideas as a group. The kids will be glad you did!

Thanks to: Orangewood Church of the Nazarene, Phoenix, Arizona

PRACTICAL WAYS TO ADDRESS SINGLE-PARENT NEEDS

There are many ways to meet the needs of single parents in your church. Your first task is to find out what those needs are. The second is to determine the resources in your church that can meet those needs. Then be creative in finding effective ways to provide support for your single-parent families. Here are some ways you might help:

1. Have a biannual clothing exchange where all families swap clothing that their children have outgrown. This can be helpful for all families, but especially for single-parent families on a tight budget.

2. Start a "Single-Parent Resources" bulletin board. Establish a visible place in your church where single parents can advertise their needs (someone to help them move or an extra bed) as well as things they have to share (a lawn mower or an oil change). In addition to the bulletin board, you may post the information in the weekly church bulletin.

3. Provide surrogate parents for special church functions such as mother-daughter or father-son outings. Plan and publicize these in such a way that surrogate parents are provided for children in families where there is no mother or father in the home. This is a wonderful way for your church members to live out Christian community and care.

4. Provide emergency baby-sitting. What happens when the child of a working single parent gets sick? Who can the parent call for help? Develop a list of people in your church who are able and willing to give emergency child care. This service would provide single parents with names of people in the church they could call to help care for their child until they get home from work.

Thanks to: *Single Adult Ministries Journal*

DATING WORKSHOP FOR PARENTS AND TEENS

Single parents with teenagers can sometimes run into awkward situations when both are dating. Kids and parents both need the opportunity to talk about mutual issues and concerns. This workshop offers a safe place to talk about what it's like to be a single parent or adolescent who is dating, or a teen who is grappling with feelings about his or her parent dating. It also presents a forum for discussing new or redefined household rules.

Questions raised in this workshop might include:

- Why do some dating rules apply to the kids and not to the parents?
- Why do kids sometimes feel insecure or uncomfortable about their parent(s) dating?
- Do parents need to answer to their children? (For example, what does a mother do when her teenage son meets her date at the door and asks "When will you have her home?" "Where are you taking her?" and "What will you be doing?"

This workshop offers an excellent opportunity for both the parents and children to talk, share their feelings, and come to a better understanding.

Thanks to: Marin Covenant Church, San Rafael, California

SINGLE-PARENT SUNDAY

The single-parent family is the fastest growing family unit in the United States. But often, people in your church may not know who the single parents are. This is an excellent way to help the entire church become more aware of the single parents in your congregation.

Designate one Sunday each year as "Single Parent Sunday." On this day, recognize single-parent families in the following ways:

1. The senior pastor acknowledges them from the pulpit, possibly asking them to stand for the congregation to recognize.

2. The two-parent families in the congregation invite the single-parent families to spend the day with them in their homes, sharing a meal, fellowship, and an afternoon/evening of getting better acquainted.

3. The singles ministry also recognizes all single parents on this day in some special way, challenging the other singles to "adopt a single-parent child" by encouraging, helping, and praying for him or her.

Thanks to: Calvary Assembly of God, Winter Park, Florida

MINISTERING TO UNWED MOMS

If you're concerned about the challenges facing the American family, then make your concern practical by reaching out to unwed mothers in your area. Unwed moms are often the poorest of America's poor, and they need a touch of human compassion and a relationship with Christ.

Locate a local house or counseling center for unwed mothers. Talk to the group's leaders about members of your group initiating one-on-one relationships and group Bible studies with the women. Then go to it.

Once your group members become involved in the lives of these women, you will become very aware that some single moms have tremendous emotional, spiritual, and financial needs. But with a little training, a lot of group discussion, and wise goals and purposes, your group will be able to minister to these moms.

Thanks to: Castle Hills First Baptist Church, San Antonio, Texas

SPIN (SINGLE-PARENT SUPPORT GROUP)

Many single adult ministries have found one of the greatest expressed needs to be a support system for single parents. One such model is called SPIN (Single Parents Internal Network).

To keep from isolating the single parents from the rest of the singles or the church, SPIN has been designed to not function as a separate singles group. Instead, it is intended to be an undergirding support system for all single parents within the overall singles ministry. The SPIN format has three thrusts:

1. A monthly workshop with speakers, testimonies, and geographically based small-group discussions for networking and building relationships.
2. A monthly newsletter with tips and helpful articles for single parents (plus a networking mailing list).
3. A one-on-one commitment among the single parents to encourage and support one another and to exchange skills and talents that can enable accountable relationships to develop.

Thanks to: South Coast Community Church, Irvine, California

LOW-COST BABYSITTING FOR SINGLE PARENTS

Why not start a program to provide low-cost babysitting at your church every Friday night? While the service could be made available to anyone in the church, consider providing special reduced rates for single parents. This regular Friday night babysitting (from 5:30 to 10:00 p.m.) will encourage and allow parents to have a breather—time for themselves that they can count on every week.

Thanks to: First United Methodist Church, Abilene, Texas

LATCHKEY KIDS PROGRAM

One way to reach out to single parents in your community is to have your church provide an after-school program for latchkey children. This program is especially effective if your church is located near densely populated apartment dwellings—a sign that there may be a high concentration of single-parent families.

The focus of this program is to provide consistent quality after-school care from 3:00 to 6:00 p.m. each day for children in kindergarten through sixth grade.

Thanks to: Grace Presbyterian Church, Houston, Texas

MAKING SINGLE PARENTS A PART OF THE CHURCH BUDGET

Scripture speaks often about the church's responsibility to care for the "orphans and fatherless." It seems only appropriate then to allot a portion of the church funds for single-parent families. This money could be used in several ways:

1. As an emergency fund designated for single parents with special financial needs.
2. As scholarship money to help single parents get a college degree so they will be better able to provide for themselves and their children.
3. As a "long-term" grant (six months to two years) to help single parents get through the roughest time of adjustment following a divorce.

Thanks to: Central Presbyterian Church, St. Louis, Missouri

FREE EYE EXAMS FOR SINGLE-PARENT FAMILIES

Many Lions Clubs across the country offer free eye exams and glasses for children from single-parent homes. Check with your local Lions Club to see if this is a service they provide in your area.

Thanks to: *Single Adult Ministries Journal*

GROUP WORK DAYS

A great way to reach out to single parents is to provide people to help with the chores that never seem to get done. Have several people from your church or singles ministry gather at the home of a single-parent family and spend the day doing repairs, yard work, painting, and so on. By holding this event several times throughout the year, you can provide a valuable service to many single-parent families in your congregation.

Thanks to: *Single Adult Ministries Journal*

BIG BUDDY PROGRAM

A "Big Buddy" program is designed to provide Christian fellowship and companionship for children from single-parent homes. Single parents who want their child to have a big buddy complete an application form and are interviewed by the coordinator to help determine needs, personality types, likes, and dislikes. A suitable big buddy is then selected for the child.

Single adults (as well as other interested persons in the church) who want to become a big buddy must commit to spend time with the child at least once a month for twelve months.

Thanks to: Wooddale Church, Eden Prairie, Minnesota

GOOD SHEPHERDS:
A MALE ROLE-MODEL MINISTRY

A male role-model ministry is an excellent way to help meet the needs of children from families headed by single mothers. It works like this:

- Recruit and develop a team of single men who enjoy children and are willing to commit a few Saturdays each year. (Depending on the number of willing men and interested children, you could schedule this day monthly, quarterly, or twice a year.)
- Advertise throughout your church each upcoming "Good Shepherd Saturday."
- Provide a convenient way for single parents to register their children to participate. (It might be a good idea to limit participation to those children who are out of diapers!)
- On the designated Saturday, single moms bring their children to the church by 9:00 a.m., dressed for outdoor activities (or whatever is appropriate for the scheduled venture), with a sack lunch and two dollars for a snack.
- Children are assigned in "flocks" to a "good shepherd." (It is best to try to keep the ratio at three to four children per adult.) After a day of fun (hiking, zoo trip, etc.), the flocks and their shepherds return to the church by 4:30 p.m.

Some of the benefits of this program are that the children get a positive male role model, single parents get a "day off," and the "good shepherds" get blessed!

Thanks to: Skyline Wesleyan Church, Lemon Grove, California

ESTABLISHING A SINGLE-PARENT RESIDENCE

This idea presents a big challenge, but offers big rewards to match.

Challenge your singles ministry or church congregation to purchase a large house or small apartment complex. If your church is unable to do it alone, consider joining forces with two or three other churches in your community. Once up and running, this facility could provide single parents the following much-needed services:

1. Low-cost rent during the first one or two difficult years of adjustment following a divorce.

2. A community and support system with other single parents in the house.

3. The opportunity to rotate child care/baby-sitting responsibilities so newly single parents can give each other a break.

The sponsoring church could also provide counseling, Bible studies, and growth groups, plus financial and career counseling in the home.

An additional option to consider with this plan is to have each single parent pay rent each month. As those payments are made, deposit the money in an interest-bearing account. At the end of twelve or eighteen months when the family moves out, make the rent plus interest available for a down-payment on a house.

**Thanks to: *Single Adult Ministries Journal*, and
East New York Church of God, Queens, New York**

WARREN VILLAGE: A UNIQUE COMMUNITY FOR ONE-PARENT FAMILIES

If the preceding idea catches your interest, but you would like to provide an even more comprehensive option, consider what one church did.

In the mid-seventies, some visionaries at the Warren United Methodist Church in Denver, Colorado, began noticing the rapidly growing number of single parents. With the help of many people from both the church and the community, they started Warren Village, a ninety-six-unit apartment building, designed for use by single-parent families. In 1984 they built a second apartment complex with 106 units.

According to NBC's "Today Show," "Warren Village is the only apartment building in the country designed specifically for the single-parent family. . . . The low-cost day care center in the building is a vital concern to the single parent. Here children can be cared for while parents pursue college or career goals. . . . Residents can get help in budgeting, child development, and career development."

Who can live in Warren Village? To be a resident, applicants must pass two screening interviews. One of the first commitments they must make is to develop an individual goal for achievement (which could include such things as education, career, or parenting skills). If residents do not work toward their self-determined goals, they can be evicted as part of the lease.

The single parent must be at least eighteen years old, have no more than four children under the age of twelve, make some income, and be eligible for subsidized housing through section eight of the Housing Assistance Payments Program.

Warren Village is not for single parents who are looking for a permanent residence, but for those who are seeking services and support that can help them gain some independence and get back on their feet again. (The average family is in residence for one-and-a-half to two years.)

What are the benefits to the resident? Aside from the sense of community that Warren's residents experience with their neighbors and the trained counselors, there are many practical benefits. For example, parents have to pay only 30 percent of their adjusted gross income for rent; the federal government pays the balance. In addition, complete professional child-care services are available in the facilities from 7:00 a.m. to 7:00 p.m. The staff helps single parents find jobs, grants, and scholarships for college, plus other information and experiences to help with personal growth. (The new village has a 15,000-square-foot computer center set up to offer services for small businesses in the community, plus provide training opportunities for village residents.)

What are the effects on the community at large? The help that single parents receive through this transition period can greatly affect their ability to contribute to the larger community. Employment and Welfare statistics provide encouraging reports: When they moved into the village, only 47 percent of the single parents were employed. After leaving, the figure rose to 94 percent. Likewise, 65 percent were receiving public assistance when they moved to Warren Village, and at departure, that figure dropped to 6 percent.

For more information, write Warren Village, 1323 Gilpin Street, Denver, CO 80218, or call (303) 321-2345. A comprehensive information and development kit, based on Warren Village's experiences over ten years, is also available to those seriously exploring a similar ministry.

Thanks to: *Single Adult Ministries Journal*

THE BREAD MINISTRY

Do you realize that many grocery stores and bakeries give away their unsold bread and pastries each week to approved nonprofit organizations?

As an extension of your single-parent ministry, why not contact your local grocery stores and make arrangements to pick up unsold bread and bakery items each week. (In many cases, grocery stores give these items away on Friday morning.)

Notify all your single parents (and other needy people in your church) to come to the church office to pick up the food on a designated day each week.

According to one singles leader, "The food supply would vary each week, but we would usually have enough food—bread, cakes, rolls, donuts—for twenty-five to fifty people. Occasionally, like at Christmas time, the stores also gave us eggnog that was still in date. And at Halloween time we received tons of candy."

Thanks to: Singles Ministry, Granby, Colorado

FREE LEGAL ADVICE FOR SINGLE PARENTS

Single parents often cannot afford the legal help they may need, but this ministry idea offers one way to give them some counsel and advice for free.

Invite a lawyer to come to your church for an evening to discuss and answer questions concerning child-custody laws, the legal rights of single parents and how to exercise those rights, and other related matters.

Advertise this evening throughout the community as a free event for anyone interested in attending. An evening such as this can provide much-needed advice for the single parents in your church and can become a bridge-building opportunity with unchurched single parents.

As an alternative, you might consider inviting a CPA for tax-related issues, a medical doctor for health matters, a banker or investment counselor for financial planning, and so on. Ask the single parents in your group what type of professional counsel they might appreciate hearing.

Thanks to: First Baptist Church, Modesto, California

THE TICKET TO ATTEND: THE SON OF A SINGLE-PARENT

The next time your church has a men-only outing (such as a fishing or camping trip), why not make it a requirement that each man who wishes to participate must bring along at least one boy from a single-parent home.

Advertise this through the church bulletin so that everyone in the church gets the message and has the opportunity to make arrangements for a boy to participate.

This church-wide event raises awareness that many children in the church are from single-parent homes. Furthermore, it regularly reminds others that single-parent children need support and modeling from adults.

Thanks to: Pinellas Park Wesleyan Church, Pinellas Park, Florida

HELP AT THE GROCERY STORE CHECK-OUT COUNTER

Many single parents who work find that their income disqualifies them from many financial assistance programs, yet their paycheck doesn't quite go as far as it needs to. Here's one way your singles can help.

Ask members of the group to pitch in to buy grocery gift certificates for struggling single parents. By providing the gift certificates instead of actual food items, the parent can choose the food his or her family prefers.

Consider offering a $50 certificate each month for three months to each single parent in the group who has special needs. The single parent will be comforted by your kindness and will appreciate knowing that for at least three months, there is an extra $50 in the food budget.

Thanks to: First Church of God, San Diego, California

SINGLE PARENTS' PERSONAL INVENTORY

Single parents sometimes can feel overwhelmed and discouraged with the course their life has taken. They need to be reminded of God's love, purpose, and plan for their lives. Here is a suggested inventory checklist to give to, or study with, your single parents. (It could also be helpful for others in your group.)

1. How does God see you? (Read Psalm 139 and Isaiah 43.) List six things from each reference that indicate how God sees you.
2. How do you see yourself? List six strengths and six weaknesses.
3. What does God expect you to do? (Read Joshua 1:5-9 and Ephesians 5:15-17.) List several expectations.
4. What does God say you can become? (See Joshua 1:8.)
5. What goals have you set for yourself? List short-term goals and when you expect to reach them. List long-term goals and when you expect to reach them.
6. What steps do you need to take to reach these goals? List a few steps for your short- and long-term goals.
7. What are some difficulties you must face in reaching these goals?
8. What can you do to overcome these difficulties?
9. What are some of the ways God wants you to minister to others? (Read Isaiah 61:1-2 and 2 Corinthians 1:3-4.) List at least six ways.

Thanks to: Belmont Evangelical Church, Chicago, Illinois

EIGHT

Finances and Fundraising

WHAT'S MINA AND WHAT'S YOURS?
(OR THE PARABLE OF THE TEN MINAS)

Do you have any people with special needs in your congregation? One pastor did. He was thinking of Jim, a single adult with eight adopted, handicapped children, who was having trouble paying his bills.

So the pastor did what anybody else would do in that situation. He took $1,000, divided it up, and gave it away in five-dollar increments to the 200 people in his congregation. What!?

That's right. He decided to reenact the parable of the ten minas found in Luke 19:12-27. Using the $1,000 as seed money, he gave five dollars to each church member and challenged them to multiply that five dollars by investing it in any way they wished.

The reaction was mixed. Some church members put their creativity to work by selling baked goods and pottery. Others organized a garage sale or lemonade stand; while still others used the seed money to print flyers advertising baby-sitting, lawn-mowing, and window-washing services. Others were less creative; they just kept the money. A few even wrote the pastor thank-you notes!

Regardless of these few failures, the experiment worked. After six weeks, the pastor collected $7,000 for Jim from his $1,000 investment! But the real value was not in the money. It was in the excitement of people accepting the challenge—help a struggling, but responsible single parent!

Thanks to: United Methodist Church, Los Altos, California

COFFEE, TEA, AND SINGLES

If your church has a coffee and fellowship time before or after the morning worship, or between multiple worship services, then this might be an idea worth trying.

Make some money for a singles ministry project and provide a nice service to the people in your church at the same time. During the morning fellowship time, have a pair of single adults stationed in the fellowship hall with urns of good quality coffee and tea and a nice selection of donuts. Ask church-goers to make a suggested donation for each item, which covers your costs, plus a profit.

Ask all the singles in your group to sign up as volunteers, then rotate them regularly so no one has to be on duty more than once a month.

The benefits of this service include helping your singles become more involved and visible in the total church. It also provides a natural, friendly way for those in your church to get better acquainted with your single adults.

Thanks to: First Presbyterian Church, Berkeley, California

"EASY PAYMENT PLAN" FOR RETREATS

If some of your people have a hard time coming up with the money to pay retreat registration fees, here's an idea that might help.

Announce the details and cost of your retreats at least five or six months in advance. Then allow your singles to use an easy payment plan over a four- or five-month period. For example, if your retreat is in July and it costs $80, ask singles who opt for the easy payment plan to send in their registration form and a $16 payment in March. Then they can pay in $16 increments during the months of April, May, June, and July. (You could even send them a bill each month if you have a computer program that makes invoicing easy.) Before they know it, the registration fee is paid—and in a less painful way!

Thanks to: First Christian Church, Amarillo, Texas

RAISING SOME DOUGH

Want to cook up a successful "dough-raising" bake-a-thon? The ingredients you'll need are singles volunteers to bake bread and get pledges, people to pledge, and patrons to buy your baked goodies. You earn money with this project from two sources: from people who pledge an amount for each loaf baked, and from people who buy the bread.

Sign up sponsors. Four weeks ahead of time, provide your singles with forms to be used in signing up sponsors.

Estimate your budget. What will it cost you to buy the ingredients for making your bread? How many loaves do you intend to make? Do you plan to wrap each loaf in some kind of bag? If yes, what are the costs? Will there be costs for a flyer to advertise your event? Put together a realistic, workable budget. (Get as many of these items donated as possible to minimize your costs.)

Establish pledge rates. For example, let's assume your group is going to bake 150 loaves of bread. Therefore, a ten-cent pledge per loaf would come to $15; a five-cent pledge would raise $7.50; a four-cent pledge would yield $6, and so on.

On the Friday night before the bake-a-thon, all the singles meet for fellowship and a fun dough-mixing time.

When the big day arrives, make sure you have the goodies arranged nicely for sale. Your singles can sign up for two-hour shifts to help on the day of the bake-a-thon. Try to get permission to sell your goods in a high-traffic area, such as in or near a mall.

At the conclusion of the bake-a-thon, make sure all sponsors receive a free loaf of bread of their choice. Each singles volunteer is responsible for giving the free loaf to his or her sponsor(s) and for collecting and turning in the pledge money to the group treasurer.

The good thing about a bake-a-thon is that, in addition to being both fun and profitable, it's also delicious!

Thanks to: Colonial Woods Missionary Church, Port Huron, Michigan

NEW FRIENDS TO THE HIGHEST BIDDER

Want a way to generate money and friendships for your group? Why not hold a "Friendship Bound" auction?

Members of the group offer services for auction: a car wash, once-a-month lawn mowing in the summer, color analysis and makeup hints, and so on. Other group members bid for the services. There are just two catches. The bidder doesn't know who it is who has offered the service, and the bidder agrees to be present when the service is performed. In this way, two people who may or may not have formed a friendship previously are brought together so one can help the other get a job done, and in the meantime, both have the chance to strike up a new friendship.

Thanks to: Alethians Singles Ministry, Faith Presbyterian Church, Aurora, Colorado; and Aeronauts Singles, Fair Oaks Presbyterian, Fair Oaks, California

(See also "Single Parent 'Tax' " on page 95.)

NINE

Service and Missions

ZOO DAY

A singles group goes to the zoo. Big deal! But when they take along local disabled kids, that's a way of mixing fun and service! You can arrange a zoo day, too. Here are some things to consider.

Organize a committee. This idea has more elements than you can handle by yourself, so start delegating right off the bat. Some people can contact all the schools and institutions that work with disabled kids and begin making arrangements for the zoo day. Others can arrange for a celebrity like Ronald McDonald to be with you. Someone else can handle zoo logistics, such as reserving picnic tables and making sure they have enough staff on hand to allow the handicapped kids to touch many of the animals.

Publicize the event. You might have someone contact all area media so that handicapped children in the community (and not only those in a school or institution) could learn about the day and get in contact with you.

Recruit singles and others who will help with all the zoo day logistics. Each child in a wheelchair will need one or two "pushers." Since many of the kids are on regular medication or may have special medical concerns, you may want to ask a few fire department medics to participate. You'll also need transportation and food for your zoo picnic. If you want, you can raise the money for the food from special offerings from your people or your church congregation.

If you're wondering what the results of all this work will be, take the word of one singles leader whose group had a zoo day, when she made this comment,

"The look on those kids' faces is worth it all."

Your zoo day may also change the lives of the singles in your group. After an experience with zoo day, the singles may be much more sensitive to and aware of people's specialized needs. An outgrowth of this may be that many single adults begin spending time with their "adopted" handicapped child one or two Sunday afternoons a month.

Thanks to: Frazer Memorial United Methodist Church, Montgomery, Alabama

PAINTING THE TOWN

You don't have to have a large singles ministry to make a difference in your community. All you need is about a dozen singles and one run-down apartment building.

Not all of your people have to be trained refurbishers, either. One or two who know what they're doing can direct those who have zeal but no experience painting or refinishing.

One group spent three consecutive Saturdays scraping and painting the stairwells, hallways, and entrances in a thirty-unit apartment building. Members of the group also contacted several people in their church and community and were able to get all the paint donated.

When all was said and done, members of the group had fun and a big achievement they could point to, and residents of the apartment building had a much-improved living environment. That's a lot for a small group to achieve in a short time!

If your city is typical, it has community or city agencies that desperately need short-term volunteer help, especially in inner-city or low-income areas. This may be an excellent way for many of your single adults to give of themselves in a practical, meaningful way.

Thanks to: First Presbyterian Church, River Forest, Illinois

SOUP AND SANDWICH HOSPITALITY

Here's a way to combine hospitality, service, and practicality in a way that benefits everybody!

Many parents find it hard to make it to church on Wednesday (or any other weekday evening) on time. They are pressed to gather up their children and get them fed. By the time they finally get to church they're fried and frazzled.

Why not have your single adults help these families by serving them soup and refreshments just before the evening church meeting? (The cost would be negligible, with the majority of the effort being in set-up and clean-up.)

One way to provide this hospitality is as follows:

1. Set up tables and a serving area in the church fellowship hall. It should be ready for arrivals approximately one hour before the church meeting(s) begins.
2. Instruct participants to bring their own sandwiches. You will provide the drinks and soup.
3. Develop a flyer advertising this service. Here's how one singles ministry explained this special service to families of the church:

FAMILIES: TAKE THIS BRIEF QUIZ

❑ Do you want to take advantage of the excellent programs offered at church on Wednesday night?

❑ Do you find it difficult to coordinate your family's schedule to get there by 7:00 p.m.?

❑ Is Wednesday supper at your house rushed?

❑ Do you hate to face dirty dishes when you come home late?

IF YOU ANSWERED "YES" TO ANY OR ALL OF THE ABOVE QUESTIONS, WE HAVE GOOD NEWS FOR YOU!

Our Singles Christian Fellowship is sponsoring a soup and sandwich supper in the Fireside Room each Wednesday evening.

WE PROVIDE: Soup & Beverage
Adults—$1.00. No charge for children 16 and under.

YOU PROVIDE: Your sandwiches, fruit, etc.

This is NOT a potluck banquet, just a "no frills" way to avoid the rush and enjoy fellowship with your Christian family. No need to sign up. Just join us at 6 p.m. for supper and 7 p.m. for our Wednesday evening church service.

Try this hospitality route with your group. It will give you a new opportunity for service and will provide some much needed relief to many of your church families.

Thanks to: Colonial Woods Missionary Church, Port Huron, Michigan

VACATIONS WITH A PURPOSE

Some people may think the phrase "vacations with a purpose" is a contradiction. After all, doesn't vacation mean "to have your brains vacate your skull," or something similar to that?

But increasing numbers of singles ministries are showing that it's possible to combine fun and world-changing ministry. Hundreds of singles are taking the time and money they would usually spend on a vacation and committing themselves to one or two weeks of work in a poor community in the United States or abroad.

The specific work these groups are doing varies. Some build churches or work at orphanages. Some help with roads or drainage. Others donate medical care or teaching skills. But regardless of the specific ministry project, there is always some time set aside for fun and sun at the end of the trip.

In order to have a successful trip, preparation is required. Travel team members attend several pre-trip classes to study foreign languages, cross-cultural ministry techniques, and team-building.

Vacationing with a purpose may be for your group if you have people who are interested in foreign missions or working with the poor. It will enrich the lives of your group members while giving them an opportunity to interact with communities in the Third World.

(For more information, start by contacting the missions office in your church or denomination. For a detailed how-to manual, get the book *Vacations with a Purpose*, published by Singles Ministry Resources/NavPress.)

Thanks to: *Single Adult Ministries Journal*

YOUR WORLD TOUR!

Today's singles—if they are anything like the national average—are geographical illiterates. So the first step in getting them turned on about missions is to make them aware of what's happening in countries around the globe.

One fun and nonthreatening way to increase your singles' awareness of the world is through a "World Tour." Here's what you do.

1. Find former missionaries and world travelers who are willing to open their homes and share their photos, slides, and experiences. Have them focus on:

- The problems faced in each country.
- What Christian workers are doing in each country.
- Each country's biggest needs.

2. Schedule a "World Tour" day. If your church is large, you may need to have a sign-up sheet to limit the number of participants. When the big day arrives, shuttle your people from house to house ("country to country"), learning about the different regions and cultures. One practical note: Give each host a time limit so

your evening doesn't last until morning!

3. After the presentations, provide refreshments (preferably authentic cuisine from one of the countries "visited") and give everyone a chance to discuss the missions needs and opportunities of the various countries.

You'll find that the act of traveling to each "country" increases the participants' interest in learning about regions of the world. The singles will enjoy learning about each country almost as much as the host enjoys talking about it!

Thanks to: Orangewood Church of the Nazarene, Phoenix, Arizona

GOD'S DESPERADOS
(GIVING ROBIN HOOD STYLE)

In the days of the old west, travelers were always on the lookout for desperados, masked raiders who appeared out of nowhere to rob unsuspecting victims. "God's Desperados" operate under a similar principle, but instead of robbing the unsuspecting victims, these mysterious, masked desperados bestow gifts!

Here are some typical ways the desperado method works:

- If you hear of someone who just lost his job, why not drop a bag of groceries on his doorstep, ring the doorbell, then run?!
- If you know someone who is sick or mourning, send him a bouquet of flowers.
- If someone's low on cash, fill her car with gas or stick an envelope with some cash in it under her door.

Once they get in the habit, desperados will pull together to do whatever it takes to help people in need. One small singles group joined together and contributed $900 to a young married couple with big medical bills.

This approach is not only tons of fun, it also gives singles training in a valuable skill: keeping their ears to the ground to learn of cases where people have needs. The key to the approach is becoming others-centered. By following the desperado method, you and your group may begin to worry less about your own problems and begin thinking more about others.

This desperados approach can be especially valuable in attracting single men and helping them build a sense of camaraderie and adventure together.

Thanks to: First Church of the Nazarene, Los Angeles, California

CAMP (CHILDREN-OF-APARTMENTS MINISTRY PROGRAM)

Our world has plenty of needs. All you need to do is open your eyes, look around, and you'll see a situation that needs compassion and care. One singles group looked to the apartment complexes in its city and what it saw was a large number of unchurched children. Many were children of single parents who couldn't give them all the love and attention they needed.

If you look around you could probably find a big apartment complex whose children your group could "adopt." Many of your singles would enjoy the chance to work with children. They can develop several teaching ministries, using formats similar to Good News Club, Backyard Bible Clubs, and Vacation Bible Schools. They can also take children to the zoo, to the countryside, or on visits to other sites in your area. Try a program of your own, and you can make a child's apartment complex almost as much fun as CAMP!

Thanks to: Castle Hills First Baptist Church, San Antonio, Texas

CAR-CARE DAY

Many singles groups are finding a practical way for their singles to help each other. "Car-Care Day" provides an opportunity for those who are less mechanically inclined to receive free car care—including tune-ups, oil changes, and minor repairs—by a group of volunteer mechanics from within the singles group or the church at large.

Your ministry can benefit from a car-care day. Here's how you can have one:

1. Schedule the day far in advance, then publicize, publicize, publicize! You will want to recruit plenty of volunteer mechanics (some of whom may need to schedule time off from work) and a lot of people who need their cars checked out.

2. Find a "pit boss," the person in your group who is the most experienced mechanic. This person will inspect the most troublesome autos, assist the junior mechanics in repairing the car, or refer the car owner to a nearby garage for more service. (If someone happens to own a computerized diagnostic unit and can bring that along, that would help greatly!)

3. Determine what you will and won't do. Avoid brake jobs, which take too long. Limiting your work to services like tune-ups, replacing hoses and belts, and oil changes should keep things moving along at a good pace.

4. Prepare a list that tells people which auto parts to bring to the clinic. This might include oil and filters, air filters, wiper blades, and other necessities. You may also want to have one or more "parts runners" who are willing to make the round trips between your "pit" and the nearest parts store.

5. Everybody can help! You don't have to know a wrench from a chassis to get involved. All you need is a willingness to help. After cars get their repairs and fix-ups, assign the less-skilled "mechanics" to wash, wax, vacuum, and further clean the cars. Pitch in to buy a few gallons of Armor All or some other protectant. The

cars can leave your lot running, looking, and smelling better.

6. Food is a must! Maybe those bringing cars for service can bring sandwiches and sodas as their "pay." Maybe a group of volunteers can sell food and donate the proceeds to the one person in your group who most desperately needs a new engine (or a new car).

If your experience is like that of other groups, your group will find that a car-care day is practical and fun, and that it helps build bridges between people who have different interests and abilities.

Thanks to: Hinson Memorial Baptist Church, Portland, Oregon; and Eastside Baptist Church, Marietta, Georgia

CARWASH WITH A TWIST

One singles group organizes a surprise carwash several times during the year. Here's how it works.

During the Sunday morning worship service, they give a free car wash to the first twenty-five couples or families who arrive at the church. The event is never announced in advance, so the carwash is a complete surprise. The singles provide this service as a way of saying thanks to the church family as well as a way to raise visibility for the single adults in the church. (It could also be a great way to encourage people to arrive on time—or ahead of schedule.)

Thanks to: Marin Covenant Church, San Rafael, California

ADOPT-A-GRANDPARENT

Your single adults may have warm memories of grandparents who have died or who live in a far-away city. Likewise, your church or city may have many elderly citizens who don't have grandchildren nearby. Why not bring the two together?

To facilitate this, each single adult is given the name and photo of a shut-in (usually a widow or widower) from the church or community. In addition to the name and photo, they are provided with information on the person's history, family, and interests. Single adults are encouraged to visit, love, and pray for their adopted grandparent on a regular basis.

If this sounds like a good idea to you, but you would like more practical information about how to form a relationship with your adopted "grandparent," consider becoming a dolphin. "The Dolphin Program" helps older and younger people form one-to-one relationships that benefit both members of the special pair. (The name Dolphin was selected for the program because of the mammal's reputation for friendship and joyfulness!)

If you would like more information on how to begin a dolphin ministry in your church or community, write The Dolphin Program, c/o St. Christopher's Church, 226 Righters Mill Road, Gladwyne, PA 19035. The telephone number is

1-215-649-5594. (A contribution of $1.50 is appreciated to cover the costs of mailing and printing the packet you will receive.)

Thanks to: First Baptist Church, Forrest City, Arkansas

FROM A SMALL SEED

Here's an easy, practical way to encourage your single adults to assist a Third World nation.

Floresta, Inc., a California-based Christian organization, plants thousands of trees in poor countries around the world to help restore both the economy and ecology. Challenge your singles group to plant "trees that last a lifetime."

For details request a free brochure: Floresta, 10855 Sorrento Valley Road, Suite 5, San Diego, CA 92121.

Thanks to: *Single Adult Ministries Journal*

START YOUR OWN SWAT TEAM

There's been a fire in the community and a home needs major repair and clean-up. A neighbor is in a car accident and doesn't have the insurance to pay for the necessary repairs. A terrible accident takes the life of a parent and the surviving spouse needs massive amounts of domestic and emotional support during the transition. Who are you going to call during difficult times like these?

One group has organized a SWAT team (Singles Working Against Tragedy) that has been there in just such emergencies. Your own SWAT team can be trained to be ready to meet adversity wherever it arises. With minimal training, and with a lot of compassion and willingness to serve, your SWAT team can be up and running, prepared for the next tragedy that may befall your community.

Your team may want to consider a weekly or monthly study on the importance of living out our faith in a world of need. Or you could take a first aid or CPR training course together. Use your imagination. What are other ways to help your SWAT team be both an effective ministry to others as well as a time of growth for those on the team?

Thanks to: East Side Church of God, Anderson, Indiana

FOOD FOR YOUR NEIGHBORS

One group has joined with local community-service agencies to help provide food for hungry families. Working with social agencies, the police, and other interested parties, they have identified families in their city who are in need of food. Since the church is in a multi-ethnic community, the singles tailor the food packages to the dietary preferences of the recipients. They also make sure that translators are available who speak the various languages in the community.

Often food is donated by individuals, restaurants, and food distributors.

The group has found that familiar food and familiar language have opened many doors of friendship and ministry. This program has also helped the group members develop an outward focus for their lives.

Thanks to: Lake Avenue Congregational Church, Pasadena, California

TEN

Surveys
and Handouts

"FAMOUS SINGLES" GROUP MIXER

There are many single adults who have made a difference—do you know who they are? Contrary to the opinions of some people, most single adults are not "sitting around waiting to be married." Many of them are making a significant difference in their world.

This mixer is a great tool to help emphasize that fact. Use it for a retreat, conference, class, or study. It will stimulate the thinking of single adults concerning their potential for achievement.

Instructions: Divide your group into teams of two. Then pass out copies of the names shown on the next page and see who can come up with the most correct match-ups in ten minutes.

Following the allotted time, have the participants share a significant goal they feel God might want them to accomplish during this year, during the next five years, or during their lifetime, and what they are doing now—or could begin doing—to help reach that accomplishment or goal.

(See "Famous Singles Quiz" on pages 122-124.)

FAMOUS SINGLES QUIZ

Who accomplished what? Match these single adults with their accomplishments listed on the next page. Not all of the names will be used.

(Find the answers on page 124.)

Hans Christian Andersen	Johns Hopkins
Susan B. Anthony	Sam Houston
Virginia Apgar	Washington Irving
Stephen F. Austin	Thomas Jefferson
Frank Ball	John Paul Jones
Clara Barton	Helen Keller
Katharine Lee Bates	Edward Koch
Emily Bissel	S. H. Kress
Elizabeth Blow	Maribeau Lamar
Dietrich Bonhoeffer	Emma Lazarus
Phillips Brooks	Amy Lowell
Jerry Brown	James Clark McReynolds
James Buchanan	Julia Morgan
Eva Burrows	Ralph Nader
Annie Jump Cannon	Flannery O'Connor
George Rogers Clark	Sam Rayburn
Grover Cleveland	Cecil Rhodes
Davy Crockett	Eleanor Roosevelt
Dorthea Dix	Christina Rossetti
Charlotte Elliott	William Scholl
Fanny Farmer	Adam Smith
Edna Ferguson	Adlai Stevenson
Felix Frankfurter	Clara Swain
Edward Gibbon	Ida Tarbell
Sarah Josepha Hale	Samuel J. Tilden
Dag Hammarskjöld	Raoul Wallenberg
Francis Ridley Havergal	Vernon Walters
George F. Händel	Anna Warner
Grace Hooper	Frank Lloyd Wright
J. Edgar Hoover	

1. _____ founded the American Red Cross.
2. _____ was secretary-general of the United Nations.
3. _____ wrote the hymn "Just as I Am."
4. _____ broke up Boss Tweed's gang.
5. _____ named 350,000 stars.
6. _____ wrote "O Little Town of Bethlehem."
7. _____ is the current general of the Salvation Army.
8. _____ pioneered research in foot care.
9. _____ raised millions for the March of Dimes.
10. _____ was a never-married U.S. president.
11. _____ was the first president of Texas.
12. _____ developed Christmas Seals.
13. _____ lobbied for a national Thanksgiving Day.
14. _____ developed a major U.S. cookbook.
15. _____ was a muckraker who exposed Standard Oil.
16. _____ rescued thousands of Jews from Nazis.
17. _____ , an economist, wrote *Wealth of Nations*.
18. _____ was Speaker of the U.S. House of Representatives.
19. _____ was the architect who designed the Hearst Castle.
20. _____ composed *The Messiah*.
21. _____ , a U.N. ambassador who gave us Rip Van Winkle.
22. _____ was a major developer of the computer.
23. _____ wrote *The Decline and Fall of the Roman Empire*.
24. _____ , a U.N. ambassador who ran twice for U.S. Presidency.
25. _____ headed the FBI.
26. _____ served on the Supreme Court for twenty-six years.
27. _____ , a gold and diamond miner who endowed scholarships.
28. _____ endowed Baltimore University.
29. _____ said, "I have not yet begun to fight."
30. _____ was the bachelor mayor of New York City.
31. _____ was the bachelor governor of California.
32. _____ , a theologian who plotted Hitler's death.
33. _____ opened the first kindergarten in the U.S.
34. _____ developed fruit jars used in home canning.
35. _____ wrote fairy tale classics.
36. _____ wrote, "Give me your poor, your tired. . . ."
37. _____ founded a department store chain.
38. _____ reformed treatment of the blind.
39. _____ wrote "America the Beautiful."
40. _____ wrote "Jesus Loves Me, This I Know."

Answers to "Famous Singles" Quiz

How well did you do? Find the correct answers below.

1. Clara Barton
2. Dag Hammarskjöld
3. Charlotte Elliott
4. Samuel J. Tilden
5. Annie Jump Cannon
6. Phillips Brooks
7. Eva Burrows
8. William Scholl
9. Virginia Apgar
10. James Buchanan
11. Stephen F. Austin
12. Emily Bissel
13. Sarah Josepha Hale
14. Fanny Farmer
15. Ida Tarbell
16. Raoul Wallenberg
17. Adam Smith
18. Sam Rayburn
19. Julia Morgan
20. George F. Händel
21. Washington Irving
22. Grace Hooper
23. Edward Gibbon
24. Adlai Stevenson
25. J. Edgar Hoover
26. James Clark McReynolds
27. Cecil Rhodes
28. Johns Hopkins
29. John Paul Jones
30. Ed Koch
31. Jerry Brown
32. Dietrich Bonhoeffer
33. Elizabeth Blow
34. Frank Ball
35. Hans Christian Andersen
36. Emma Lazarus
37. S. H. Kress
38. Helen Keller
39. Katharine Lee Bates
40. Anna Warner

Source: Adapted with permission from the book
A *Singular Devotion*, by Harold Ivan Smith (Revell, 1990)

SPIRITUAL GROWTH SURVEY

If you want to know what your singles want, ask them. The following survey isn't exhaustive, but it can be an efficient, effective way to find out more about some of the spiritual growth opportunities your singles are looking for, as well as what program possibilities exist.

SINGLES SPIRITUAL LIFE SURVEY

1. I would be interested in (check one or more):
   - ❑ Beginner's Bible study group
   - ❑ Advanced Bible study group
   - ❑ Prayer group
   - ❑ Sharing group
   - ❑ Spiritual growth group
   - ❑ Other _____

2. I would prefer to meet with (check one):
   - ❑ Men only
   - ❑ Women only
   - ❑ Men and women

3. A convenient time for me to meet is:
   - ❑ Sunday 8:30 a.m.
   - ❑ Sunday 9:30 a.m.
   - ❑ Sunday 11:00 a.m.
   - ❑ Sunday afternoon, time_____
   - ❑ Sunday evening, time_____
   - ❑ Weekday morning before work, time_____
   - ❑ Weekday, early evening, time_____
   - ❑ Saturday, time_____

Add to the survey by incorporating questions you want to ask your singles. Print plenty of copies and hand them out during your regular meeting or insert them in the church bulletin.

Thanks to: Peachtree Road United Methodist Church, Atlanta, Georgia

MALE-FEMALE SURVEY

Here is an excellent way to generate interest in an upcoming retreat (or weekend seminar). Distribute the survey that follows (or one like it) to the singles in your church and community. Announce in advance that the results of the survey will be presented at the retreat. (It would be ideal if the teaching at the retreat also tied in to the survey topic.)

The survey is intended to stimulate discussion and to help single adults understand what men and women most value in a person of the opposite sex.

To help reach unchurched singles in your community, distribute the survey to as many single adults as possible. Put all the details of the retreat on the survey: when, where, cost, topic, and so on. Make it clear that the results will be announced at the retreat. This will serve as a wonderful way to advertise the weekend event. A lot of folks might turn up just to find out more about this male-female mystique!

Thanks to: Central Presbyterian Church, St. Louis, Missouri

(See "Male-Female Survey" on next page.)

MALE-FEMALE SURVEY

This questionnaire will give you the opportunity to say to members of the opposite sex, "These are the things that I, as a man or woman, value in my relationships with members of the opposite sex."

Instructions: From the list of fifty attributes, pick the top ten items according to your own personal values and write them in the spaces provided below. Rank them in order of your personal preference, with the letter A assigned to your most important value, the letter B to your second most important, and so on. It may be difficult to pick only ten from the list of fifty choices, but do your best. (Be honest! We want to know what really is important to you. You do not need to give your name.)

A. _____   F. _____

B. _____   G. _____

C. _____   H. _____

D. _____   I. _____

E. _____   J. _____

CHOICES

1. Intelligent
2. Sense of humor
3. Handsome/pretty
4. Well proportioned
5. Compassionate
6. Good listener
7. Good sexual partner
8. Self-starter
9. Outgoing
10. Adventuresome
11. Sensitive
12. Ambitious
13. Dresses well
14. Spiritually strong
15. Mature
16. Emotionally warm
17. Common interests/ goals
18. Committed to me
19. Close friend
20. Romantic
21. Social sophistication
22. Affectionate
23. Financially secure
24. Reliable/trustworthy
25. Well educated
26. Athletic
27. Good physical health
28. Emotionally stable
29. Playful
30. Well groomed (physically)
31. Active in church
32. Forgiving
33. Doesn't drink/smoke
34. Loves children
35. Pursues me
36. Accepts me as I am
37. Good communicator
38. Independent
39. Enjoys quiet things
40. Needs me
41. Is growth oriented
42. Has many other friends
43. Likes to travel
44. Strong personality
45. Easygoing
46. Morally pure
47. Respects me
48. Shy
49. Flexible
50. Giving

HOW HEALTHY IS YOUR SUNDAY SCHOOL CLASS?

Are your single adults having their needs met in your Sunday school class or Bible study group? Is your class or group inviting? What is it about a class or study group that makes adults want to attend?

According to author Alan Tungett, there are three primary reasons adults attend Sunday school or Bible study groups:

Fellowship. The words loving, caring, accepting, belonging, and security describe this best. For many adults, fellowship is the primary reason for attending Sunday school.

Meaningful Bible study. The focus here is on "meaningful"—teaching the Bible with an emphasis on people and their needs.

Spiritual atmosphere. Tungett says, "A spiritual atmosphere is generated when Christians talk freely with one another about the difference Sunday's Bible study makes in their daily living. . . . It centers on what leaders and members do with what they have been taught."

Below is an evaluation form to test the atmosphere of your singles Sunday school class or Bible study. Discuss the results with your leadership team. Together, determine how you can improve your single adult class.

Survey

How descriptive of your single adult class or study group are the following sentences? Write the appropriate number in the space provided: 1 for "very descriptive," 2 for "somewhat descriptive," or 3 for "not descriptive."

A. Members know one another. _____
B. Members have a sense of belonging. _____
C. Members have and show a personal interest in one another. _____
D. Members experience exciting Bible study. _____
E. Members share personal experiences, feelings, and concerns. _____
F. Members make newcomers and visitors feel welcomed
   and accepted. _____
G. Members have and show a sense of appreciation for one another. _____
H. Members are supportive of one another. _____
I. Members share their faith with others. _____
J. Members help one another when there is need. _____
K. Members express Christian love for one another. _____
L. Members take the initiative in greeting and meeting new people. _____
M. Members accept responsibility for relating to outsiders. _____
N. Members participate in growth-producing activities. _____
O. Members bring their friends to Sunday school and/or
   Bible study. _____

Adapted from *Sunday School Leadership* magazine, September 1983

INDEX CARD SURVEY FOR PROGRAM PLANNING

What subjects should you address in your singles TNT group meetings? (TNT is a week-night discussion group popular among many singles groups across the country. TNT stands for "Tuesday Nights Together" or "Thursday Nights Together." Another similar group is called TIO—"Talk It Over.") Here's one way to keep tabs on TNT or TIO group interest and needs.

Take a quick poll of the members of your group by using this simple survey on an index card once each month (see sample below). The information can provide guidance to your planning committee as they develop the programs for the future. This provides an opportunity for the entire group to have a voice in the kinds of topics and programming for your meetings.

TNT SURVEY CARD

We want to learn about some of the things that you are interested in having for our Tuesday Nights Together evening program, *providing practical helps for living*. Please check the items that you would most like to hear about:

- ❏ car repairs and maintenance
- ❏ yard care, mower, planting, etc.
- ❏ clothing repairs and simple alterations
- ❏ household repairs
- ❏ decoration ideas for you home
- ❏ buying a home on a budget
- ❏ other (name it):_____

What "repair," skill, or expertise can you share with the group? Tell us about it on the back of this card.

Suggestions/comments _____

_____

_____

Your name_____

Phone_____

**Thanks to: Singles Ministry,
Gulf Breeze United Methodist Church, Gulf Breeze, Florida**

INVOLVEMENT SURVEY

The survey on the following page is a great way to start a data base on the people who regularly attend your group. It will give you finger-tip access to who is coming to your group, why they're coming, what they can offer you, and what they'd like to be offered in return.

Be sure to adapt this survey to fit your needs.

Why use this survey? Involvement generates commitment. The more involved your single adults are, the more they will sense personal ownership in—and enthusiasm for—the ministry. The challenge is to find a meaningful job for every person in your singles group. This survey is designed to find out who in your group has the time and interest to serve in a particular job, as well as to learn about each person's interests and skills.

As a steering committee, brainstorm every possible way someone could become involved in your group. List all possible activities (such as sports and socials), logistical problems (setting up chairs and tables), Bible study groups, committees that need members—anything and everything in which someone's skills and abilities might be used.

How often should this survey be given? Give it two or three times each year so the class stays aware of needs and opportunities. (It would also be helpful to give this survey to all new class members.)

What should you do when the survey has been completed? Make certain that one of the leaders contacts each person the following week. If the follow-up is not done promptly, people will think the group really does not need them. The benefits from something so simple as this are fantastic.

Thanks to: Northwest Bible Church, Dallas, Texas

(See "Involvement Survey" on pages 131-133.)

SINGLES MINISTRY INVOLVEMENT SURVEY

Your name_____

Home phone_____ Work phone_____

Address_____

City_____ State_____ Zip_____

Please indicate your response:

1. How often do you attend this singles class?
   ❏ Every week ❏ Twice a month ❏ Once a month ❏ Visitor
2. Are you interested in being in a "care group" that enables the members to have weekly contact by phone or in person? ❏ Yes ❏ No

**Please let us know which of the following
you would be willing and able to participate in:**

1. Assist with physical arrangements for each class (weekly):
   ❏ Yes ❏ No
2. Assist with decorating tables for potluck dinners (twice a month):
   ❏ Yes ❏ No
3. Musical accompaniment for singing: ❏ Yes ❏ No
   Which instrument do you play?_____
   Have you had any experience in leading songs/music? ❏ Yes ❏ No
4. Assist with helping our singles move out of or into another apartment or house. (This generally involves Saturdays, once a month maximum.)
   ❏ Yes ❏ No
   Sometimes; call me first: ❏ Yes ❏ No
5. Assist with producing our monthly newsletter: ❏ Yes ❏ No
6. Serve as a greeter or welcome-table helper each week: ❏ Yes ❏ No
7. Visitor follow-up (call and/or send a card): ❏ Yes ❏ No
8. Assist with prayer list requests and answers (keeping a journal):
   ❏ Yes ❏ No
9. Hospital visitation committee (occasional visits): ❏ Yes ❏ No

(Continued)

10. Assist with planning socials and activities: ❑ Yes   ❑ No
11. Take responsibility to assist and/or teach a Bible lesson to children of single parents during some of our meetings on a rotating basis:
    Teach a lesson: ❑ Yes   ❑ No
    Assist in some other way: ❑ Yes   ❑ No
12. Be involved in a weekly Bible study: ❑ Yes   ❑ No
    What evening and time is best for you?
    Evening _____ Time _____
13. What two topics would you like to see our group study/discuss/address in the upcoming months?
    First topic:_____

    Second topic:_____
14. I would like to serve on the missions committee: ❑ Yes   ❑ No
15. I would like to serve on the care committee: ❑ Yes   ❑ No
16. I would like to be a weekly prayer partner with someone of the same sex in this group (weekly phone contact or meeting for prayer):   ❑ Yes   ❑ No
17. I would like to head up and coordinate or assist a committee that helps others in finding jobs (receive résumés, get the word out, make needs known):
    I would be glad to be in charge of coordinating this area:
    ❑ Yes   ❑ No
    I would be glad to assist someone in this area: ❑ Yes   ❑ No

Other ways to provide ministry to this group:
 1. I have access to a pickup truck that could be used occasionally to help people move: ❑ Yes   ❑ No
 2. I have some skill related to my job that others might benefit from; i.e., "I am a CPA and would be glad to assist group members with their taxes."
    Skill:_____
 3. I would be glad to be contacted before a retreat or seminar to assist in offering money for scholarships for those who cannot afford to go otherwise: ❑ Yes   ❑ No
 4. I would be glad to share my testimony during some upcoming class: ❑ Yes   ❑ No
 5. I would be glad to help with home needs such as car tune-ups, mowing grass, painting projects, fix-up needs: ❑ Yes   ❑ No
    Types of projects:_____
 6. I have some typing skills and would be glad to assist in typing résumés or other needs you may have (from two to three hours per month maximum):
    ❑ Yes   ❑ No   *(Continued)*

7. I would be glad to do something else to minister in some practical ways to folks involved in this group: ❑ Yes   ❑ No
   List your area(s) of expertise:

   _____

   _____

   _____

   _____

   _____

   _____

   _____

Other comments/suggestions:

_____

_____

_____

_____

_____

_____

_____

Thanks for taking the time to complete this survey!

MINISTRY IS YOU AND ME

People would like to think that a minister is someone we pay to help us. But the Bible teaches that we are all ministers to one another.

Here's a helpful tool to bring home the reality—or the inadequacy—of our ability to minister to each other. This will enable each of your singles to think through and evaluate his or her own ministry and responsibility to others in the group.

Duplicate the sentences below on another sheet and leave adequate space for responses. Distribute the questions in a Sunday school class or Bible study group and ask each person to complete each sentence anonymously. Complete the responses and use them as a springboard for class discussion the following week.

1. One thing I give to this class is . . . .
2. One thing I do to harm this class is . . . .
3. Visitors to our class probably see me as . . . .
4. I show Christlikeness in this class by . . . .
5. One thing I can do to improve my ministry in this class is . . . .

You may also want to add other incomplete sentences that go further in describing the level of mutual ministry in your group.

Adapted from *Youth Leadership* magazine, April-June 1985

Index

YOUR IDEAS
ARE WORTH UP TO $100!

If you have ideas that have worked well in your own singles ministry, we want to let others know. We are already collecting ideas for future editions of *The Idea Catalog* and would love to have your input. If we use your idea, we will pay up to $100. Please send a thorough description of your idea (along with your name, church, address, and phone number) to:

IDEAS
Singles Ministry Resources
P. O. Box 60430
Colorado Springs, CO 80960-0430